T0210757

Transaction Processing on Modern Hardware

Synthesis Lectures on Data Management

Editor
H.V. Jagadish, *University of Michigan*

Founding Editor
M. Tamer Özsu, *University of Waterloo*

Synthesis Lectures on Data Management is edited by H.V. Jagadish of the University of Michigan. The series publishes 80–150 page publications on topics pertaining to data management. Topics include query languages, database system architectures, transaction management, data warehousing, XML and databases, data stream systems, wide scale data distribution, multimedia data management, data mining, and related subjects.

Transaction Processing on Modern Hardware
Mohammad Sadoghi and Spyros Blanas
2019

Data Management in Machine Learning Systems
Matthias Boehm, Arun Kumar, and Jun Yang
2019

Non-Volatile Memory Database Management Systems
Joy Arulraj and Andrew Pavlo
2019

Scalable Processing of Spatial-Keyword Queries
Ahmed R. Mahmood and Walid G. Aref
2019

Data Exploration Using Example-Based Methods
Matteo Lissandrini, Davide Mottin, Themis Palpanas, and Yannis Velegrakis
2018

Data Profiling
Ziawasch Abedjan, Lukasz Golab, Felix Naumann, and Thorsten Papenbrock
2018

© Springer Nature Switzerland AG 2022

Reprint of original edition © Morgan & Claypool 2019

All rights reserved. No part of this publication may be reproduced, stored in a retrieval system, or transmitted in any form or by any means—electronic, mechanical, photocopy, recording, or any other except for brief quotations in printed reviews, without the prior permission of the publisher.

Transaction Processing on Modern Hardware

Mohammad Sadoghi and Spyros Blanas

ISBN: 978-3-031-00742-2   paperback
ISBN: 978-3-031-01870-1   ebook
ISBN: 978-3-031-00097-3   hardcover

DOI 10.1007/978-3-031-01870-1

A Publication in the Springer series
SYNTHESIS LECTURES ON DATA MANAGEMENT

Lecture #58
Series Editor: H.V. Jagadish, *University of Michigan*
Founding Editor: M. Tamer Özsu, *University of Waterloo*
Series ISSN
Print 2153-5418   Electronic 2153-5426

Transaction Processing on Modern Hardware

Mohammad Sadoghi
University of California, Davis

Spyros Blanas
The Ohio State University

SYNTHESIS LECTURES ON DATA MANAGEMENT #58

ABSTRACT

The last decade has brought groundbreaking developments in transaction processing. This resurgence of an otherwise mature research area has spurred from the diminishing cost per GB of DRAM that allows many transaction processing workloads to be entirely memory-resident. This shift demanded a pause to fundamentally rethink the architecture of database systems. The data storage lexicon has now expanded beyond spinning disks and RAID levels to include the cache hierarchy, memory consistency models, cache coherence and write invalidation costs, NUMA regions, and coherence domains. New memory technologies promise fast non-volatile storage and expose unchartered trade-offs for transactional durability, such as exploiting byte-addressable hot and cold storage through persistent programming that promotes simpler recovery protocols. In the meantime, the plateauing single-threaded processor performance has brought massive concurrency within a single node, first in the form of multi-core, and now with many-core and heterogeneous processors.

The exciting possibility to reshape the storage, transaction, logging, and recovery layers of next-generation systems on emerging hardware have prompted the database research community to vigorously debate the trade-offs between specialized kernels that narrowly focus on transaction processing performance vs. designs that permit transactionally consistent data accesses from decision support and analytical workloads. In this book, we aim to classify and distill the new body of work on transaction processing that has surfaced in the last decade to navigate researchers and practitioners through this intricate research subject.

KEYWORDS

transaction processing, ACID semantics, consistency, isolation levels, concurrency controls, optimistic concurrency, pessimistic concurrency, multi-version concurrency control, hardware-conscious concurrency, HTAP, indexing, hardware acceleration, RDMA

To Lili Taghavi
–Mohammad Sadoghi

To my family
–Spyros Blanas

Contents

CHAPTER 1

Introduction

The need to process transactions motivated a lot of the early research in database systems. Back in the 1970s, transaction processing research encompassed multiple components: data entry from geographically distributed terminals, networking technology to meet stringent time requirements to update the database, and database management systems that were continuously available to minimize downtime. As technology evolved over several decades, the constituent parts of a transaction processing system were tasked to support new application needs. Data entry terminals sparked research into user interfaces and visualization, interconnecting heterogeneous networks paved the way for the development of the Internet, and database systems research shifted its focus to querying massive databases for reporting and decision support purposes. At the turn of the century, research activity in transaction processing had slowed down significantly as other application needs captured the attention of the research community.

Instead of transitioning to obscurity, as many other research topics have throughout the years, research interest in transaction processing rekindled around 2010. At this time, startups and established vendors started offering specialized database systems that promised to accelerate transactional performance by one order of magnitude or more. This change did not go unnoticed by researchers, who proposed new research prototypes of their own that exclusively targeted transaction processing workloads.

We are now witnessing the renaissance of transaction processing. Interest in transaction processing has spread to multiple research communities. The database systems community is investigating new storage and indexing methods, as well as ways to more tightly integrate concurrency control and data storage for higher performance. The operating systems community is considering methods to optimize distributed transactions and minimize coordination. The distributed systems community is investigating how to run transactions on geo-replicated databases where consensus on the fate of a transaction can be reached through a quorum. This book aims to distill this new body of work and make it approachable to practitioners and researchers that are new to this field.

1.1 THE SHIFTING HARDWARE LANDSCAPE

With the benefit of hindsight, the spark of research interest in transaction processing can be attributed to two trends in the hardware landscape that profoundly impacted the design of database systems.

TREND #1: LARGER, CHEAPER MEMORY

The first hardware trend impacted the memory subsystem. The cost and the capacity of memory, both off-chip and on-chip, significantly changed during the last decade. Figure 1.1 shows the cost of DRAM per GB and the capacity of the last level cache of CPUs in the Intel Xeon family. One can observe the following.

1. The cost of DRAM per GB decreased by nearly 100× between 2006 and 2016.

2. Since 2005, the last level of the CPU cache is increasing by 10 MB every two years.

TREND #2: MORE, NOT FASTER, CPU CORES

The second hardware trend is the end of Dennard scaling. As manufacturers could no longer drastically raise clock frequencies between every generation of a CPU, they invested the increasing transistor budget to add CPU cores. Figure 1.2 shows the base frequency and the CPU core count of CPUs in the Intel Xeon family. One can observe the following.

1. Since 2005, the base CPU frequency has been increasing by about 0.1 GHz every two years.

2. The period between 2005–2014 has seen the addition of 2.5 more CPU cores every two years on average. Since 2014, the pace has accelerated to 8 more CPU cores every two years.

IMPLICATIONS

The implications of these trends on the design of database systems is profound.

- **Many transaction processing databases fit entirely in memory.** The affordability of DRAM means that many transactional databases can be stored entirely in memory. This necessitates a redesign of the data storage and recovery methods of a database system.

- **Small databases are becoming cache-resident.** With cache sizes reaching many MBs, many small databases are becoming cache-resident. Inefficiencies on the compute path, such as branch mispredictions or underutilization of the vector units of a CPU, have now a significant impact on performance.

- **Hardware upgrades alone will not meaningfully improve transaction processing performance.** The uncharacteristically slow pace of clock frequency growth means that existing database systems will see marginal performance improvement from hardware upgrades when the entire database fits in memory. Transaction processing systems need to reduce the number of instructions they execute per transaction to keep up with the pace of data growth. In particular, redundant components such as a buffer pool manager need to be removed from the code path for memory-resident databases.

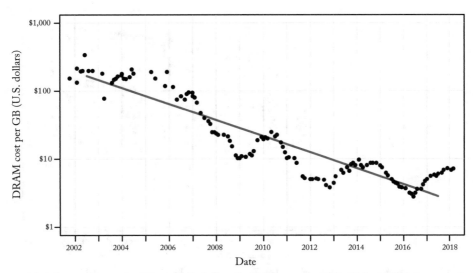

(a) Memory cost per GB in U.S. dollars [86]. The cost of DRAM per GB decreased by nearly 100× between 2006 and 2016.

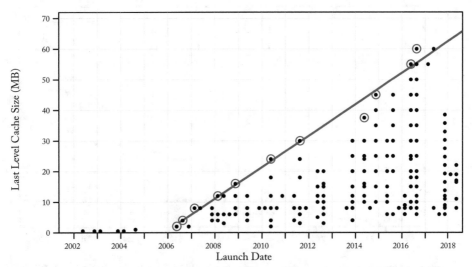

(b) Size of the last level cache in CPUs of the Intel Xeon family [53]. The capacity of the last level CPU cache has increased by 10 MB every two years since 2005.

Figure 1.1: Historical data on memory cost and CPU cache size.

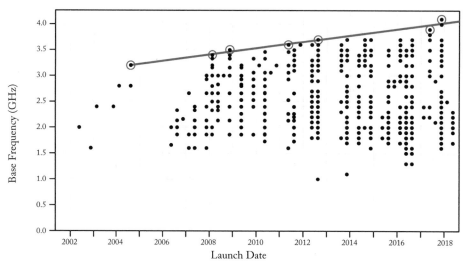

(a) Base frequency of CPUs of the Intel Xeon family [53]. The base CPU frequency has been increasing by about 0.1 GHz every two years since 2005.

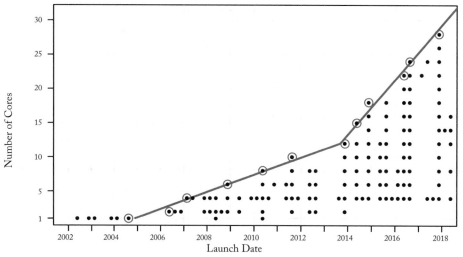

(b) Number of cores in CPUs of the Intel Xeon family [53]. The period between 2005–2014 has seen the addition of 2.5 more CPU cores every two years on average. The pace has accelerated to adding 8 more CPU cores every two years since 2014.

Figure 1.2: Historical data on CPU frequency and CPU core count.

- **Transaction processing systems need to leverage on-chip concurrency to continue to scale.** Transaction processing systems need to explicitly specify what tasks can be executed concurrently by multi-core and many-core CPUs. The engineering effort that is required to extract and expose parallelism to the hardware is often comparable to designing a new database kernel.

1.2   BOOK OUTLINE

Chapter 2 describes basic terminology for transaction processing, and introduces the concepts that subsequent chapters will build on. Chapter 3 introduces new research in multi-version concurrency control, including optimistic and pessimistic variants. Chapter 4 presents techniques that are designed to avoid coordination. Chapter 5 discusses novel system architectures for transaction processing. Chapter 6 describes common mechanisms to accelerate transaction processing, in particular, partitioning and indexing methods. Chapter 7 presents recent research in hardware-conscious data stores, with special emphasis on hardware heterogeneity. The focus is on how transaction processing can leverage hardware accelerators and network capabilities like RDMA. Finally, Chapter 8 presents exciting challenges that lie ahead.

CHAPTER 2

Transaction Concepts

In this chapter, we cover the fundamental concepts of transaction processing in databases, which is essential to appreciate the later chapters.

2.1 OVERVIEW

What is a transaction? Why a transaction is needed? What are the desired properties of a transaction? How do we process transactions efficiently? These questions are at the core of data management systems that facilitate the digitalization of contracts or agreements among a set of individuals, parties, or entities. The term "transaction" is defined as follows.

Definition 2.1 A transaction is an instance of buying or selling something or an exchange or interaction between people.[1]

A transaction can be viewed as an exchange of goods or services among individuals. A transaction can be further generalized as performing a set of actions or operations over shared resources or, alternatively, managing shared resources or data among entities. A transaction can also be viewed more abstractly as an exchange or alteration of shared states among entities.

To formalize transactions, we define a set of basic properties that any transaction ought to satisfy [15, 44, 45]. Essentially, formalizing how to manage shared resources while allowing many entities to concurrently access and alter shared resources. One way to ensure correctness, the expected or desired behavior, is to categorize a set of unwanted side-effects or anomalies. Executing each transaction may alter the state of shared resources or data, which we refer to as the *effect* or *outcome* of a transaction. To further elaborate on the effects of transactions, we could say that its effects are either fully applied or dismissed altogether (i.e., *atomicity*).[2] Once the effects of the transaction are applied, then it should never be forgotten (i.e., *durability*). One could further describe how the effects of transactions are actually applied. For example, we must ensure that applying a transaction does not violate any rules, constraints, or invariants imposed on the state of shared resources, or in another word does not violate the integrity of shared resources (i.e., *consistency*). Lastly, if we were executing multiple concurrent transactions, then we must also ensure there are no conflicting concurrent actions (i.e., *isolation*).

---

[1]Oxford Dictionaries: https://en.oxforddictionaries.com/definition/transaction.

[2]Metaphorically, a transaction is viewed as an indivisible set of actions meaning, either all or none of the actions must succeed, which is based on the early belief that atom is the smallest possible unit and that is indivisible or irreducible.

The notions of atomicity and durability are desired properties of transaction, while consistency is the property of whether the transaction's net effects are permissible or whether the violates a desired set of rules or constraints. The concept of isolation is the property of the operational semantics, not a property of transaction per se, in order to avoid undesired effects or anomalies. Although these properties focus on different aspects of transactions, we generally refer to them as transaction semantics, and collectively referred to them as transactional **ACID** properties: **A**tomicity, **C**onsistency, **I**solation, and **D**urability [15, 44, 45].

2.2   ACID PROPERTIES

Now that we have given the basic intuition behind a transaction, we are ready to formalize the concept of transactions and ACID properties.

In the database literature, a transaction T_i in its simplest form is defined *as a set of operations over shared data that transforms the data from one consistent state to another.*[3] Each operation is either a read of data item x, denoted by $read_i(x)$ or $r_i(x)$, or a write to a data item x, denoted by $write_i(x)$ or $w_i(x)$. For example, a transaction that reads x and y and writes z can be written as $T_i = \{r_i(x), r_i(y), w_i(z)\}$ implying the partial ordering of operations such that $r_i(x) \rightarrow r_i(y)$ and $r_i(y) \rightarrow w_i(z)$, whereby $r_i(x) \rightarrow w_i(z)$ is implied by transitivity.

2.2.1   ATOMICITY

The transaction boundary is often denoted by BEGIN or END, where the ending of transaction could take many forms such as COMMIT that indicates success, or ROLLBACK or ABORT that indicates failure and the need to reverse any changes made by the transaction.[4] Once the transaction commits, then all of its effects must be reflected on the new state of the database. When a transaction aborts, then none of its effects should be reflected and any partial changes of states must be rolled back to the initial state before the transaction began.[5] The transaction atomicity property ensures the all or nothing criteria, implying either all transaction operations are executed successfully and the database is transitioned into a new consistent state or none is executed and the database remains in the original state.

2.2.2   CONSISTENCY

A database $\mathcal{D}$ can be defined by the triple $\mathcal{D} = \{\mathcal{S}, \mathcal{I}, \mathcal{C}\}$. The schema $\mathcal{S}$ is the meta-data that defines a set of relations or tables, where each relation is a set of columns or attributes. The database instance $\mathcal{I}$ is the shared data that conforms to the schema $\mathcal{S}$, simply a set rows or tuples

---

[3]This definition can be generalized by defining the transaction as a partial ordering of operations or nested transactions. Although a useful notion, it has received little attention from the research community in the recent years due to the limited practical use.

[4]Partial commits or rollbacks are also supported by most commercial database vendors.

[5]Here we simply assume no concurrent transactions or no visibility of uncommitted data to concurrent transactions, otherwise cascading aborts may occur for any transaction that reads data from an aborted transaction.

per relation. Additionally, a database may define a set of integrity constraints $\mathcal{C}$ to determine if database instance $\mathcal{I}$ is consistent or not, namely, a set of rules for assessing the soundness of the data, e.g., account balance should not be negative.

The operational semantics of the database $\mathcal{D} = \{\mathcal{S}, \mathcal{I}, \mathcal{C}\}$ can be defined by the state transition $\mathcal{I}_j \xrightarrow{T} \mathcal{I}_{j+1}$, where the transaction T transforms the database from an initial consistent state $\mathcal{I}_j$ to a new consistent state $\mathcal{I}_{j+1}$. Therefore, the **C** in ACID is focused on state consistency, namely, whether data remains consistent after executing a transaction [2].

2.2.3 ISOLATION

Any system that grants execution of only one transaction at a time over shared resources trivially satisfies isolation properties because interleaving of operations from different transactions simply does not take place. Therefore, only when interleaving of operations is permissible, then there is a need to reason about the correctness of the final outcome to account for conflicting operations. In other words, how the work of one transaction is *isolated* or *protected* from other concurrent transactions. Enforcing isolation is to ensure the correctness of operational semantics.

One way to reason about the correctness is to permit operation interleaving as long as it can be mapped to some serial execution of transactions. In a serial schedule, the conflicting transaction T_i occurs either before or after the transaction T_j. This forms the basis of database *serializability theory* that formalizes the correctness (or the safety criteria) of execution of concurrent transactions. For example, one way to ensure the serializability is to maintain strict isolation among transactions, in a sense dividing shared data into disjoint pieces (a set of one or more items) and each piece is assigned to one transaction. Now if a transaction cannot secure its own piece it has to wait or if multiple concurrent transactions have mutual interests in the same piece of data, then only one should be granted access.

In general, the concurrency control (CC) mechanism is responsible to satisfy the correctness of the operational semantics. The goal of CC protocols is to facilitate coordination among transactions to ensure correct ordering of operations to reach a valid final state. The concurrency mechanism achieves desired isolation semantics either by proactively (i.e., pessimistically) preventing or ordering conflicting operations during the execution or by passively (i.e., optimistically) identifying conflicting operations or conflicting state before a transaction can commit and make its changes visible. Irrespective of the concurrency choice, the net effects of a transaction must be serializable or satisfy other well-defined weaker semantics.

The classical isolation theory is often characterized in terms of to what degree concurrent transactions are shielded from one another as far as conflicting operations are concerned. For example, when can we expose the write of an active transaction (uncommitted partial work) to other active transactions, referred to as *the visibility criteria*. An uncommitted write can be both be read (referred to as *dirty read*) and/or over-written, referred to as *dirty write*, essentially creating *dependency* between the first writer transaction and concurrent reader and/or writer transactions who subsequently access it. If after an active transaction reads a data item the data is overwritten by a concurrent transaction, then this leads to what is referred to as *non-repeatable read*. This creates an *anti-dependency* between the reader transaction and the concurrent writer transactions who subsequently modify the shared data. If after an active transaction reads a predicated range of data items and then a concurrent transaction inserts a new item or deletes an item that falls within the predicated range, this leads to what is referred to as a *phantom*; in a sense, creating a phantom data item with respect to the original reader that would be visible (or invisible if it was deleted) if the reader re-fetches the range.

The degree to which concurrent transactions are isolated from one another during the execution is also referred to as the degrees of consistency [45] which are formalized as follows.[6]

- *Degree 0 Consistency* offers the least degree of isolation that allows both *dirty reads* and *dirty writes*. It prevents partial reads and offers atomic writes (i.e., operation atomicity).

- *Degree 1 Consistency* prevents *dirty writes* (cf., *Read Uncommitted*).

- *Degree 2 Consistency* prevents *dirty writes* and *dirty read* (cf., *Read Committed*).

- *Degree 3 Consistency* prevents *dirty writes, dirty read, non-repeatable read, phantom* (cf., *Serializable*).

The concepts of *dirty write, dirty read, non-repeatable read,* and *phantom* are also known as *phenomena* or *anomalies* that may arise due to weak isolation. Isolation semantics are often characterized by whether they are able to avoid these anomalies.

Other well-known anomalies are *lost update, read skew,* and *write skew*. Lost update occurs when a transaction T_i reads a data item x and subsequently T_i writes to x and commit. Now if the write operation of T_j is interleaved between $r_i(x)$ and $w_i(x)$, then we say the write $w_j(x)$ is a lost update because $w_i(x)$ is based on a stale value of x. This is an example of such a problematic schedule: $H = r_i(x), w_j(x), w_i(x), c_i$. The *read skew* anomaly occurs when a transaction only observes partial writes of a concurrent transaction, namely, reading an inconsistent state that is never possible in a serializable schedule. For example, $H = r_i(x), w_j(x), w_j(y), c_j, r_i(y)$. The *write skew* anomaly occurs when there is an implicit (or hidden) constraint between two data items x and y. Transaction T_i reads x but updates y while transaction T_j does the reverse, it reads y and updates x. Essentially, the juxtaposition of reads and writes: $H = r_i(x), r_j(y), w_i(y), w_j(x), c_i, c_j$

The final subtle point that may arise due to weak isolation is what happens when some transactions are aborted and whether the effects of their partial work can be reversed. In particular, when transactions are allowed to read dirty data, they become dependent on the transactions that changed the data. There is a possibility that a writer transaction is aborted, thereby all of its changes are rolled back and now all the dependent transactions are also forced to abort. However, if a dependent transaction is allowed to be committed based on the dirty data of an

---

[6]Despite the tremendous success and commercial impacts, the degree of consistency formulation and ANSI SQL has been the subject of wide criticisms, causing ambiguity for both researchers and practitioners.

aborted/rolled back transaction, then the wrongfully committed transaction is no longer valid or *recoverable*.[7] Thus, to ensure recoverability, a dependent transaction should either avoid reading dirty data or delay its commitment until all the transactions on which it depends on also committed (*wait dependency*). The latter choice may result in what is called *cascading aborts* because one abort may trigger a chain reaction to abort all dependent transactions.

Another commonly used weaker semantic is snapshot isolation that ensures all reads of the transaction are based on the image of the database in an instantaneous point in time, often chosen to be the start time of the transaction.

2.2.4 DURABILITY

According to durability criteria, after a transaction is committed and its effects are applied, namely, moving the database from an old state to a new one, then the new committed state must never be lost in the case of failure. In other words, the committed state must always be recoverable after a crash (e.g., node or media failures). Durability is often achieved by maintaining undo and redo logs, where the log is the history of all changes made to the database, retaining the order in which they were applied reflecting the commit order. Essentially, an ordered undo and/or redo actions.

Conceptually, the undo log is used to reverse the modifications of any aborted transactions, which is to ensure that no partial or uncommitted data are retained after a crash, with no data corruption, while the redo log is used to reapply modifications of committed transactions, which is to ensure that all committed data are retained after a crash, with no data loss. The log could be either physical, i.e., keeping track of the physical changes to each data item or a set of data items (e.g., at the page level), or logical, i.e., tracking the operations performed on data.

2.3 CONCURRENCY CONTROL OVERVIEW

A simple way to avoid anomalies, due to conflicting actions by concurrent transactions, is to execute transactions serially. However, executing transactions one after another leads to poor performance. This has led to the creation of what is known as *transaction serializability theory* that defines serial execution as the gold standard—what is deemed to be a correct execution. This theory defines a transaction history as a partial order schedule as the history of (partial) ordering of transactional actions/operations. A serial execution trivially satisfies conflict-free execution because only one transaction is executed at any time, resulting in a serial history. Therefore, viewing serial execution as the basis, the serializability theory characterizes a correct execution of concurrent transactions. It defines an ordering as an execution of history that can be mapped to a possible serial execution.

---

[7]Unless complex and expensive compensation routine is invoked to revoke or fix the wrongfully committed state. A common example is the airline double booking of the same seat.

Conflict–serialize schedule imposes a partial ordering only on conflicting operations among concurrent transactions that map to a serial schedule;[8] the more restrictive *strict conflict-serializable schedule* imposes a partial ordering only on conflicting operations among concurrent transactions that map to a serial schedule that abides by real-time order (i.e., wall clock) of issued transactions; and the even stricter *linearizable schedule* imposes a total order among transactions that abides by real-time order, namely, it does not permit any interleaving of transaction operations and views all operations within a transaction as a single atomic action that is applied instantaneously.

2.4   OVERVIEW CONCURRENCY CONTROL PROTOCOLS

There have been countless concurrency control protocols proposed over the last few decades [15], but the interest in this classical problem has recently been revived by both industry (e.g., [28, 40, 73, 77, 110–112, 115, 116, 123]) and academia (e.g., [40, 55, 57, 62, 64, 79, 95, 103, 108, 111, 122, 128, 129, 131, 134, 146]) due to hardware trends (e.g., multi-cores and large main memory) and application requirements (e.g., millions of transactions per second in algorithmic trading). As far as concurrency control is concerned, a database system can be broken down to few simple components, as demonstrated in Figure 2.1: concurrency control protocols, execution threads, data, index, and log.

We characterize concurrency control behavior as either pessimistic or optimistic depending on how reads are validated, as shown in Figure 2.2. The pessimistic approach validates the reads before reading while the optimistic approach validates the reads only before committing the transaction. An orthogonal, but crucial, aspect for both pessimistic and optimistic protcols is whether a transaction waits for the validation, i.e., whether the concurrency protocol relies on locking (blocking) or not (non-blocking).

Orthogonal to both pessimistic and optimistic paradigms is the basic idea of assigning a timestamp to transactions and ordering a transaction based on time either as part of execution or during validation. The timestamp ordering (T/O) assigns a monotonically increasing timestamp (either a physical clock or a logical clock such as a counter) to each transaction. In the basic version of T/O [14], each data item tracks the timestamp of the last transaction that accessed it; a separate read and write timestamps may also be maintained for each record to further increase the concurrency (e.g., [146]). When a transaction attempts to access a record, the request is not granted if the record timestamp is greater than the transaction's timestamp.

Broadly speaking, on the one hand, we classify concurrency control mechanism as either pessimistic or optimistic and, on the other hand, we classify them as being either coordination-free, i.e., an attempt to drop the need for any CC protocols, or restrictive concurrency, i.e., tailored and limited to specific workload properties, such as partitionability. Such a classification is a daunting task and does not offer a strict dichotomy because there is a tremendous degree of overlap among many of these approaches, and many of these protocols can be extended to

---

[8]This can easily be verified if the dependency graph of the transaction history/schedule is acyclic.

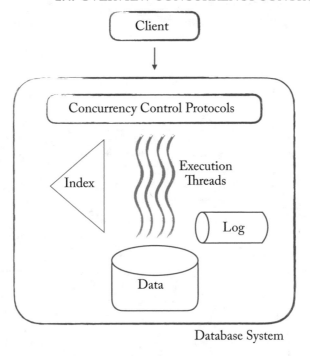

Figure 2.1: A high-level overview of a transactional system.

support both optimistic and pessimistic paradigms [73, 112]. Nevertheless, we make an attempt to offer such classification, presented in Figure 2.3, as a first step to paint a big picture and bring more unity and clarity to this complex and exciting field.

2.4.1 PESSIMISTIC CONCURRENCY CONTROL

Generally speaking, the traditional pessimistic concurrency control has validate, read, and write phases. Validation can be classified as either fine-grained locking (individual records) or coarse-grained locking (disjoint sets of records). There is often an implicit computation step between the read and write phases, where one executes the transaction logic which determines what operations to execute next or how to compute the value to be written, as captured in Figure 2.2.

Two-Phase Locking Techniques (Fine-Grained Locking). The standard two-phase locking protocol (2PL) is based on the idea that the transaction execution is divided into distinct two phases: a growing phase in which locks are strictly only acquired followed by a shrinking phase in which locks are strictly only released. The 2PL is the first instance of a CC protocol to be formally proven to ensure serializability [17, 35]. Over the years, there have been many proposed locking variations, e.g., [14, 108, 112, 134], all focused on central questions of how to

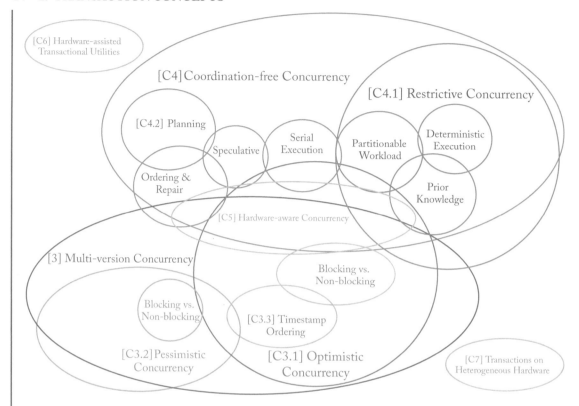

Figure 2.2: Validations in concurrency control protocols.

reduce locking contention, the contention between readers and writers, or how to avoid dead-locks. Section 3.2 review recent advancements in this front.

Partition Locking (Coarse-Grained Locking). Instead of viewing the database as a set of individual records, one can view the database as a set of disjoint partitions, namely, disjoint sets of records. Therefore, the concurrency protocol issues locks for a partition of the data as opposed to acquiring locks on the individual records. The root of these ideas dates back to hi-erarchical locking, where one may issue an (exclusive) lock on a record, page, region, table, or the entire database [45]. A recent manifestation of this idea is seen in H-Store [57], where data is partitioned into a set of disjoint partitions (and as long as all transaction data falls within a partition, i.e., partitionable workload), then simply all transactions are ran serially within each partition without a need to have any concurrency control during the execution. Each partition is implicitly locked, and each transaction is granted an exclusive access to an entire partition. Such an execution paradigm will achieve nearly optimal performance if the workload is partitionable; however, once a transaction data span multi-partition, then the performance may sharply drop to an unsustainable rate [145].

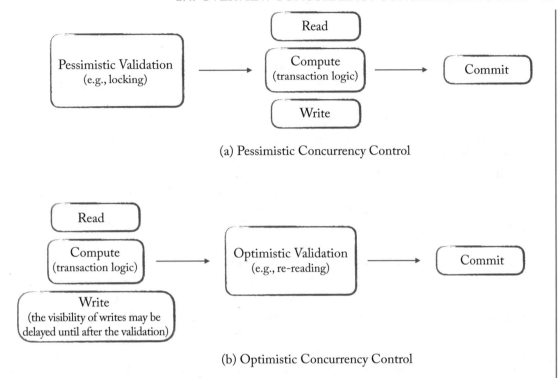

(a) Pessimistic Concurrency Control

(b) Optimistic Concurrency Control

Figure 2.3: Concurrency control protocol classification.

2.4.2 OPTIMISTIC CONCURRENCY CONTROL

The optimistic paradigm simply drops the need to validate the reads proactively by acquiring locks. It generally follows a three-phase protocol of read, validate, and write [69]. A more general reformulation is to first perform read and write in addition to the implicit compute phase with an option to make the writes only visible after the validation (as shown in Figure 2.2). In reality, the question of write visibility is really the question of whether allowing dirty reads/writes and not whether the execution is optimistic or pessimistic. Most optimistic concurrency controls (OCC) are required to track the read and write sets and maintain a private working space (to avoid early write visibility) for each transaction. At the time of validation, the readset is cross-checked against the writesets of all concurrent transactions to ensure read stability [69] or all the records in the database are read again to ensure their values have not been changed [73, 112]. To ensure the atomicity, in the validation phase both the readset and/or writeset are often locked. If the validation is successful, then the transaction can commit and writes are made visible and all changes are applied to the database.

DISCUSSION

Although in the database literature consistency refers to the fact that no constraints are violated, in the distributed systems literature consistency defines the operational semantic correctness, namely, whether the net effects of a transaction are correctly applied to all shared data including any replicated data while preventing any anomalies due to conflicting concurrent transactions. Generally speaking, the notion of consistency in a distributed system is closely aligned with the isolation semantics in databases. To make the matter more complicated, the different database isolation levels are also characterized as an increasing degree of consistency ranging from allowing both dirty (uncommitted) read/write to serializability.

To partially resolve this ambiguity, we may adopt an alternative viewpoint that states **I** in ACID is focused on operation consistency [2], namely, whether a desired level of isolation is achieved when executing concurrent transactions. While **C** is concerned with the state consistency by formalizing what constitutes a valid state, i.e., limiting the degree of change to data, **I** is concerned with operation consistency by formalizing what constitutes a valid execution sequence or a valid schedule, i.e., limiting the degree of freedom to interleave concurrent transactions.

Another challenge with our current formulation of isolation levels is that it mixes the concept of isolation with its implementation mechanism. As it was also implied in [1], our definition of attaining the desired level of isolation is highly biased toward the pessimistic mechanism that has adopted a locking protocol. The concurrency control mechanism itself can further be defined as either state or operation consistency. The latter imposes an explicit ordering of operations, perhaps using locks, to achieve a desired isolation (potentially maintaining a consistent partial state at all times). While the former is often characterized as optimistic and does not necessarily impose any constraints on interleaving of operations (potentially having inconsistent partial states), it does require the final state to be validated before accepting and committing the changes made by a transaction.

CHAPTER 3

Multi-Version Concurrency Revisited

There exists a rich body of research on concurrency control techniques, including several classic books on the subject (e.g., [12, 68, 127]). In the past decade the interest in multi-version concurrency control protocols has revived, leading to the development of numerous novel approaches. To close this gap, this chapter first focuses on optimistic protocols, followed by covering the pessimistic approaches. A section is dedicated to time ordering concurrency that is applicable to both optimistic and pessimistic techniques. The chapter concludes by examining a contention-free storage architecture necessary to maintain the multi-version data model.

3.1 OPTIMISTIC CONCURRENCY

3.1.1 HEKATON

As part of the Microsoft Hekaton project, Larson et al. [28, 73] re-examined the cost of failed optimism, that is to allow reading/writing of the data without guarding it and only at the commit time realizing that data were invalidated by concurrent transactions. Of course, any invalidation will result in aborting and rolling back the transaction. But a keen observation was that the cost of aborting and retrying a transaction is becoming increasingly cheaper because data is now memory-resident and the disk I/O can be virtually eliminated from the critical path of a transaction [28, 73]. Therefore, there is a compelling argument as to why one should develop costly and complex pessimistic techniques for proactively identifying and resolving conflicts when one can simply retry the problematic transaction. Hekaton introduced a redesigned transaction manager that completely avoids the use of a lock manager and relies on copy-on-write and read validation techniques to ensure repeatability while performing re-execution of all range queries to achieve phantom protection and serializability. It heavily relies on the atomic compare-and-swap (CAS) instruction of a CPU to support latch-free data structures. For example, write-write conflicts are detected by atomically swapping record's timestamp and aborting the second writer to avoid blocking.

Hekaton's original data structure utilizes an unclustered hash table for storing the data in the main memory. Its data model is demonstrated in Figure 3.1, in which the schema is assumed to be known at the table creation time. It consists of the following meta-data fields: (1) begin and end timestamps on which CAS operation are applied to ensure access atomicity; (2) a pointer to the next version of the record; (3) a pointer to the next element in the hashed bucket (note that the closed addressing is employed with chaining to deal with collisions); (4) index links, a predefined pointer for each secondary hash index defined on the table, which is needed to enable closed address chaining; and (5) the actual data fields.

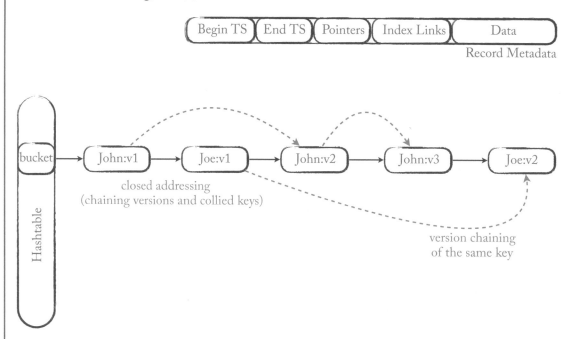

Figure 3.1: Hekaton data model.

Hekaton's proposed transaction state diagram is presented in Figure 3.2. Each transaction begins by reading and writing data in a speculative mode. If no write-write conflict is encountered while the transaction completes all of its read and write operations, it enters the preparation phase at which point a final timestamp (a commit time) is reserved from a synchronized monotonically increasing global clock, arguably the only synchronization point in the system. Once the commit time is known, then all the reads are validated accordingly, and upon the successful validation, logs are forced to disk, the transaction is committed. Any post-processing tasks, such as reflecting the commit time in all modified records, are lazily completed.

The Hekaton in-memory storage was further extended with cold persistent storage as part of the Siberia project by Eldawy et al. [32]. Siberia's architecture is demonstrated in Figure 3.3, which offers a framework to manage cold data. It provides the necessary machinery to migrate data from hot to cold storage (and back) while transactions can continue reading and writing the cold data consistently. The migration process and tracking of the modification to the cold data revolve around the idea of a scratch book. This is an update memo space in which the data in transition between the two storage modes are tracked.

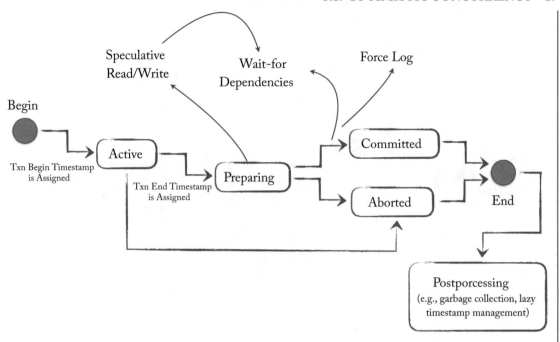

Figure 3.2: Hekaton optimistic transaction model (state transitions).

3.1.2   HYDER

Bernstein et al. [13, 16] introduced Hyder, a non-partitioned, scale-out architecture that is centered around a shared log. Conceptually, Hyder can be viewed as a fully replicated system, in which each node independently maintains a copy of the data. Each copy is a multi-version snapshot of data that is reflective of transactions recorded in the shared log and eventually becomes consistent with the log through what is referred as a *log-roll forward* routine. Hyder eliminates the need for traditional agreement protocols to reach consensus by enforcing atomic append to the shared log before the fate of the transaction is determined independently by each replica.

As demonstrated in Figure 3.4, each transaction is optimistically executed by a replica based on its latest local copy of the data (possibly not reflecting all the recorded and committed transactions on the shared log). Once a transaction is fully executed, but not yet committed, it creates a single *intention* record that includes its readset (if serializable isolation is desired) and the after-image of its writeset. The intention record is broadcasted to all replicas and written atomically to the shared log. The atomic write ensures the total ordering of the log, and once the log record is written, its offset is broadcasted to all replicas (including the replica that produced the intention record). Since the intention log and its offset are shared with all replicas, each node can independently construct an image of the log locally and roll forward the log to determine the fate of each transaction (commit or abort) based on the position of its intention record

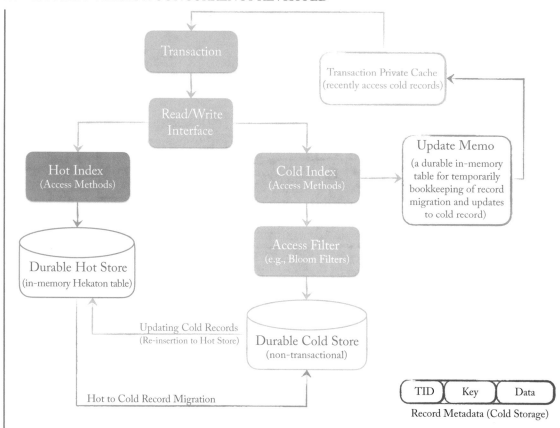

Figure 3.3: Extending Hekaton with a cold storage layer.

in the log. A consistent commit decision is made independently by each replica without any coordination. The process of detecting transaction conflicts is referred to as melding the log. For each intention record, the melding process identifies a potential conflict zone of recently written intention records that were not reflected in the local snapshot of the replica at the time when the transaction was executed.

3.1.3   2VCC: TWO-VERSION CONCURRENCY CONTROL

Sadoghi et al. [112] introduced a two-version concurrency control (2VCC) protocol that allows the co-existence of both pessimistic and optimistic concurrency protocols, all centered around a novel indirection layer [115, 116] that serves as a gateway to locate the latest version of the record and a lightweight coordination protocol to implement both blocking and non-blocking behaviors in the face of conflicts. Before diving into the concurrency aspects, we first explain the indirection idea and its variant that are central to the understanding of the 2VCC protocol.

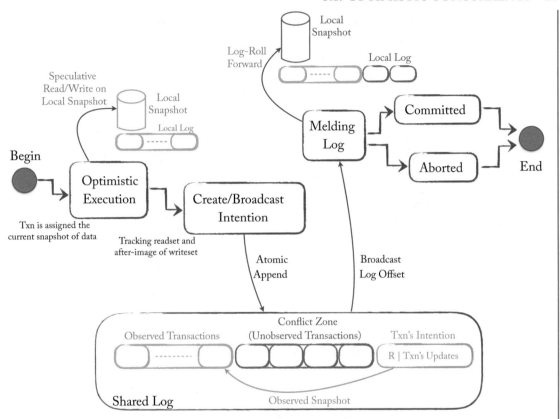

Figure 3.4: Hyder optimistic transaction model (state transitions).

One way to envision the indirection layer is to extend the storage hierarchy (optionally using a fast non-volatile memory such as SSDs) with an extra level of indirection in order to *decouple the logical and physical locations* of the records [115, 116]. This was primarily designed to overcome the index maintenance cost in a multi-version database. This is especially instrumental in a multi-version data store that retains the history by avoiding any in-place updates. In such a setting, the cost of index maintenance becomes a major obstacle to cope with the velocity of change to data.

By incorporating the indirection mapping, illustrated in Figure 3.5, the traditional RID-based indexes[1] are replaced by LID-based indexes, and, thus, a RID-to-LID translation is necessary that is carried out using the indirection layer. The indexes now store the stable logical identifier of each record, instead of changeable RIDs which are changed every time a record is updated with a copy-on-write policy. By traversing the indirection layer, the actual physical

---

[1]RID (Record Identifier) is the pointer to the physical location of the record.

location of the record is determined. As a result, random updates to all indexes are eliminated and only the indirection mapping and the indexes on modified columns are now affected due to record modifications. This simple approach substantially reduces the cost of maintaining indexes.

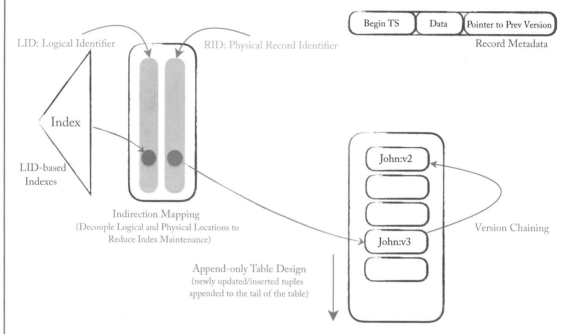

Figure 3.5: **2VCC** data model (indirection mapping).

The idea of indirection focuses on address decoupling while granting direct access to the latest version of the record with an extra look-up, but it does not address how to manage storing an actual change to a record. Sadoghi et al. [116] introduced the delta block to augment indirection and track recent changes to the record. As shown in Figure 3.6, each LID-to-RID mapping slot is extended with delta space to store the actual modifications to the record. Instead of performing copy-on-write of the entire record for each update, the deltas are stored along with the mapping. Periodically, once the delta space is filled, the deltas are flushed and a new version of the record along with its recent history is flushed to the table space.

The delta block idea is manifested in three forms captured in Figure 3.7. The *direct deltablock* technique explicitly extends and stores the actual deltas (a fixed space extension) within the indirection mapping slot; *indirect deltablock* extends and stores only pointers to deltas (a fixed set of pointers extension) within the indirection mapping slot, and it uses a scratch space to buffer the recent deltas; *indirect, chained deltablock* extends and stores only a pointer to the latest delta (a single pointer extension) within the indirection mapping slot, and it assumes a scratch space to buffer recent deltas, where deltas of the same records are chained with a backpointer to the previous delta.

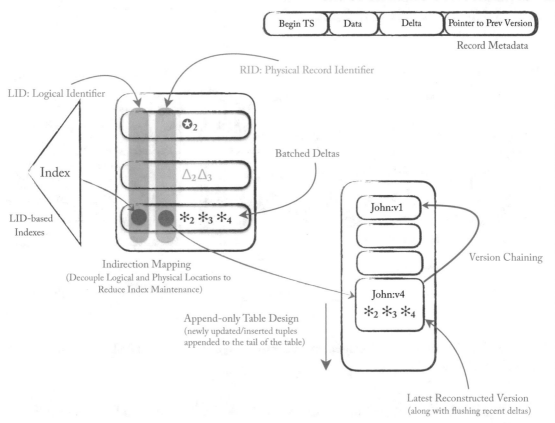

Figure 3.6: Indirection batching recent updates.

The indirection idea is further extended to distinguish between a committed RID (cRID) and an uncommitted RID (uRID) for each record (i.e., k-indirection), facilitating the decoupling of readers and writers traversing indexes, a step toward eliminating read/write contention (as shown in Figure 3.8) [112]. For example, the readers will follow the committed RID route while the writers will follow uRID and subsequently update it if null. If the uRID is set, it implies an outstanding update on the record, which is an eager indication of write-write conflict; if the uRID is not set, then the writer appends the new version of the record to the table (copy-on-write scheme) and updates uRID accordingly. Once the writer commits, the uRID and cRID are swapped and uRID is set to null, signifying that there are no outstanding writes on the record. The uRID may optionally hold a read counter, tracking how many outstanding readers have read the currently committed version of the record. This allows a latch-free coordination mechanism among readers and writers for read stability.

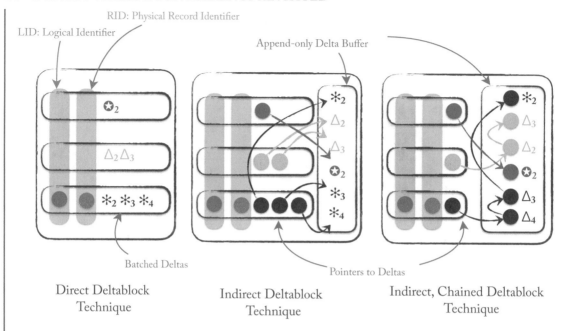

Figure 3.7: Indirection delta management: direct deltablock, indirect deltablock, and indirect chained deltablock techniques.

Recall that in operational multi-version databases there is a tremendous opportunity to avoid clashes between readers (scanning a large volume of data) and writers (frequent updates). To close this gap, a (latch-free) 2VCC was proposed in [112]. It extends the indirection mapping, i.e., a central coordination mechanism, and exploits existing 2PL in order to decouple readers and writers to reduce contention. This further enables pessimistic and optimistic concurrency control protocols to co-exist by exploiting the indirection as a light-weight bookkeeping system.

The basic idea of 2VCC [112], illustrated in Figure 3.9, is similar to the traditional 2PL that consists of growing (acquiring all necessary locks) and shrinking phases (releasing any locks). Next, the protocol is expanded by introducing a certify phase, a reminiscent of 2V2PL proposed in [15]. Therefore, at the outset of a transaction both readers and writers will only acquire shared locks, and once the transaction completes all its operations, it will promote its shared locks to exclusive locks (namely, certifying its writes) for any modified records. Notably, the actual change to the record is done prior to entering the certify phase, and the new location of the uncommitted record is also announced through the indirection layer using the uRID.

The certification ensures that there are no outstanding readers of currently committed versions so as to ensure read repeatability. Thus, exclusive locks held for a shorter period are limited to the certify phase. The approach is inherently optimistic because it presumes any out-

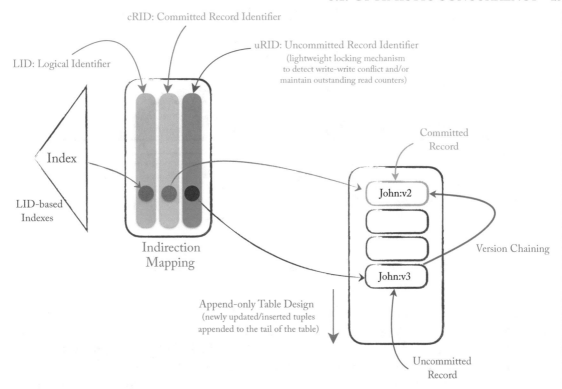

Figure 3.8: 2VCC data model (k-indirection mapping).

standing readers have completed before entering the certify phase; this, in fact, offers a way to introduce structured optimism. Waiting can be a fallback to allow draining the outstanding readers at commit time. A further optimization is to discover inevitable write-write conflicts that are impossible to resolve pre/post-commit time, unless restricting the kind of writes (e.g., commutative operations such as increment or decrement) or adopting complex post-commit compensation routines. To detect a write-write conflict, the writers request a special *update lock* instead of shared locks, which signifies the intention to change the data in the traditional relational design. Note that with update locks in 2VCC the actual record is changed and a new version is added which is accessible through the indirection layer. Alternatively, the conflict can be detected using a lock-free approach implicitly by atomically setting the uRID using the CAS instruction upon copy-on-write.

Thus far, we have focused on how to improve optimism when it comes to write operations while following a strict pessimistic read paradigm. To allow another form of structured optimism, the readers can be allowed to speculatively read the uncommitted version when outstanding writers are completing their certify phases, a strong indication that those writes will

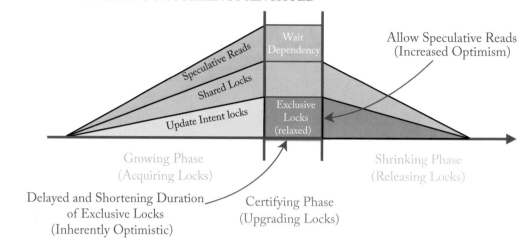

Figure 3.9: 2VCC transaction model (pessimistic and optimistic transitions).

successfully certify and commit since they have eagerly identified all write-write conflicts before entering the certification. Lastly, the trade-offs between blocking (i.e., locks) vs. non-blocking (i.e., read counters through indirection layer) are exploited in 2VCC, some of these strategies have already been alluded to using uRID optimization. The intuition behind the co-existence of pessimistic and optimistic protocols is directly related to how both the blocking and the non-blocking schemes are leveraging the indirection layer [112].

3.1.4   CENTIMAN: OPTIMISTIC WATERMARKING

Ding et al. [29] proposed a new optimistic concurrency approach based on a decomposed system model designed with elastic scaling in mind. The underlying architecture (shown in Figure 3.10) revolves around loosely coupled, non-transactional key-value stores on different nodes, which simply serve as stable storage with fine-grained atomic access. The actual task of preserving transactional semantics are carried by the compute and validator nodes. The compute node is what drives the transaction logic, receives client requests, and buffers recent writes before pushing them to stable storage. The validator nodes, each responsible for a portion of data, carry out the validation phase and buffer the recently validated and committed writes to speed up the process.

The two main synchronization points are in the proposed Centiman protocol [29]. At the start of the validation phase (a necessary step for any optimistic concurrency control scheme), synchronization is needed in order to acquire a globally consistent commit time, analogous to Microsoft Hekaton [28, 73]. But unlike Hekaton, the validation is carried in a distributed fashion and without redoing reads. Thus, a second synchronization is needed, in which the compute node responsible for the transaction needs to collect the decisions from all validators to reach the

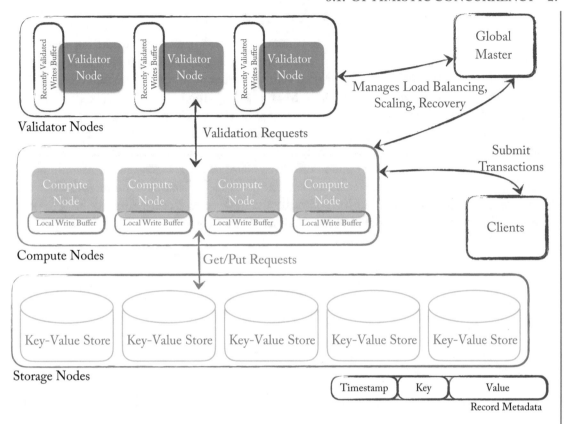

Figure 3.10: Centiman elastic optimistic concurrency control architecture.

final outcome, closely resembling the two-phase commit logic. To communicate the outcome of transactions among nodes, Centiman introduces a watermarking technique to compute and disseminate the timestamp of the latest committed transaction[2] while the transaction writes are propagated asynchronously to the stable storage. Thus, each validator is assigned an exclusive partition of data, validates operations in strict commit order and remembers the recent writes it has validated. By knowing the high watermark of the latest committed transactions, Centiman reduces spurious aborts due to maintaining only partial validation information and not knowing the final fate of transactions that validated successfully locally but failed in another validator.

---

[2]Lazy propagation of the high watermark only results in an increased chance of spurious aborts and does not violate serializability.

3.1.5   HYPER: A HYBRID OLTP AND OLAP DATABASE

Neumann et al. [95] aimed to retain single-version scan performance by introducing a fast optimistic multi-version concurrency control that adopts in-place updates, maintains an undo buffer of a recent overwritten delta, and relies on a validation that acquires a consistent commit time from a synchronized global clock (similar to Microsoft Hekaton [28, 73]) that avoids maintaining the readsets of all transactions by instead employing a precision locking variant in which explicit read locks are essentially replaced with predicated range locks indexed by a predicate tree [95, 113]. As demonstrated in Figure 3.11, the underlying structure is extended with a version column that points to the last undo buffer that changed the records, closely resembling the indirection and delta approaches introduced earlier [115, 116]. Each undo buffer is dedicated to a unique transaction holding all of its modifications. Each undo buffer references back to other undo buffers (if any) holding the previous versions of the record.

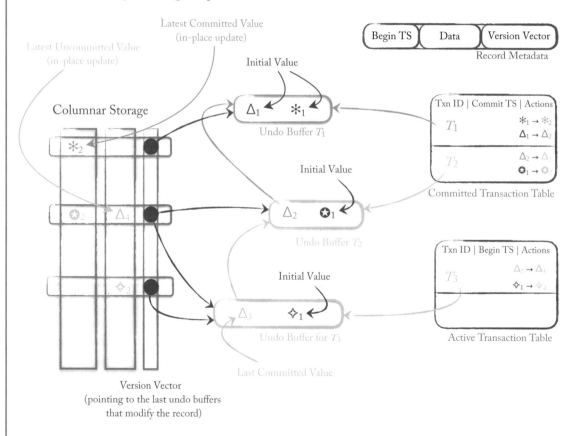

Figure 3.11: HyPer multiversion concurrency control architecture.

3.1.6 ERMIA

Kim et al. [62] presented ERMIA, a memory-optimized database system offering a certifier-based optimistic concurrency control that is centered around (1) the indirection mapping to serve as latch-free, low-overhead coordination mechansim [115, 116], (2) an epoch-based resource management [110, 111], and (3) a serializability-enforcing certifier based on the serial safety net (SSN) certification [133]. The EMRIA architecture is provided in Figure 3.12. From the data layout perspective, only LID-based indexes are employed and EMRIA relies on the indirection mapping to retrieve both the latest and earlier versions of each records. The core of the execution is carried out in two phases: (1) a forward processing phase in which all transaction footprints (e.g., writes) are visible only locally and skipped by other active transactions; and (2) a pre-commit validation phase in which commit LSN is obtained, changes are flushed to a central log buffer, and SSN certification is invoked (cf. Section 3.3.4).

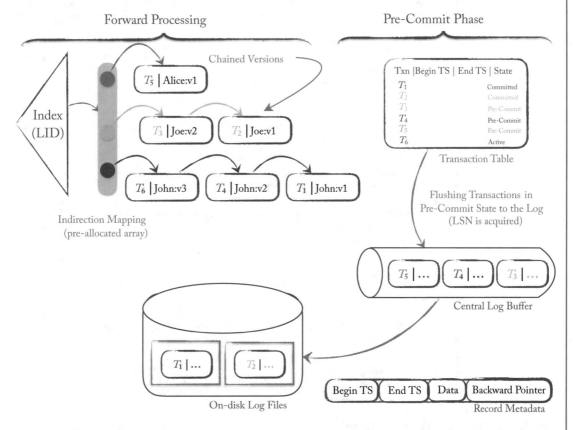

Figure 3.12: **ERMIA** transaction lifecycle and architecture.

3.1.7   CICADA

Lim et al. [79] introduced Cicada, a fast in-memory data store equipped with an optimistic concurrency control that is serializable and mitigates the costs associated with multi-versioning and contention challenges by carefully examining various layers of the system. The Cicada protocol is captured in Figure 3.13, and offers several general optimizations that can be applied to most optimistic protocols: (1) employing an early abort check during the read phase to eagerly determine the likely scenarios that would result in aborting the current transaction, for example, detecting write-write conflicts where there is an outstanding competing writer in the process of being validated ahead of the current transaction;[3] (2) the validation sorts the writes based on the degree of contention, namely, examining the hot records that may trigger an abort first; and

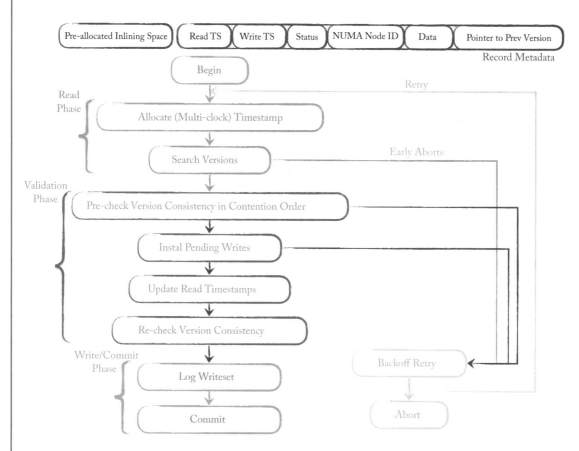

Figure 3.13: Cicada MVCC protocol.

---

[3]Notably, the early write-write conflict detection is an effective optimization that is adopted in other recent concurrency protocols such as [28, 62, 111, 112].

(3) a contention regulation model based on a backoff scheme using the hill climbing technique to determine the optimal maximum retry time for aborted transactions.

3.1.8   SPECULATIVE MULTI-PARTITION TRANSACTIONS

Jones et al. [55] extended H-Store's simple single-threaded execution model that is optimized for single-partition transactions and eliminates the need for any concurrency protocol (cf. 4.1.1) [57]. To support multi-partition transactions, a speculative execution model is introduced such that as soon as a multi-partition transaction T_i completes on one partition (i.e., commits pending confirmation from other sites), the partition begins to execute any outstanding transaction in speculative mode such that their commit is pending the success of T_i. In the spirit of stepping away from having any concurrency protocol, no read-write sets or locks are maintained during speculative execution (thus all subsequent transactions are assumed to be conflicting), only an undo buffer is maintained that is needed to recover from cascading aborts of all speculative transactions if T_i is aborted. As shown in Figure 3.14, as soon as *Node 1* receives the final fragment of T_1, Step (2), the speculation begins. Although there is no need to run a concurrency ordering protocol, the proposed model still requires an agreement protocol, e.g., two-phase commit, to reach consensus among all partitions.

3.1.9   BCC: BALANCED CONCURRENCY CONTROL

Yuan et al. [147] presented balanced concurrency control (BCC) that unlike existing optimistic protocols offers a tighter validation condition in order to reduce the false abort rates. The basic tenet follows that the readset violation during the validation step is not a sufficient condition to blindly abort a transaction because a true serialization violation arises only when there is a cycle in the transaction dependency graph. BCC introduces a tighter bound on the definition of unserializable schedule by searching for essential patterns that are necessary and sufficiently stronger condition to detect validation violation in comparison to the standard readset validation. BCC dictates that the essential pattern may form a cycle in which at least one of the edges is a write-after-ready anti-dependency, as demonstrated in Figure 3.15.

3.2   PESSIMISTIC CONCURRENCY

3.2.1   SLI: SPECULATIVE LOCK INHERITANCE

To reduce the contention of the lock manager on many-core machines, Johnson et al. [54] proposed the speculative lock inheritance (SLI) technique in which hot locks are passed on from one transaction to the next. The new transaction inherits the lock without the need to interact directly with the lock manager, and no release or acquire calls are needed. Essentially, the agent thread that is responsible for executing the transaction will selectively hold locks (presumably hot) once its current transaction is completed and it will pass on the locks as needed to the next transaction assigned to it, as shown in Figure 3.16. SLI is particularly effective for hierarchi-

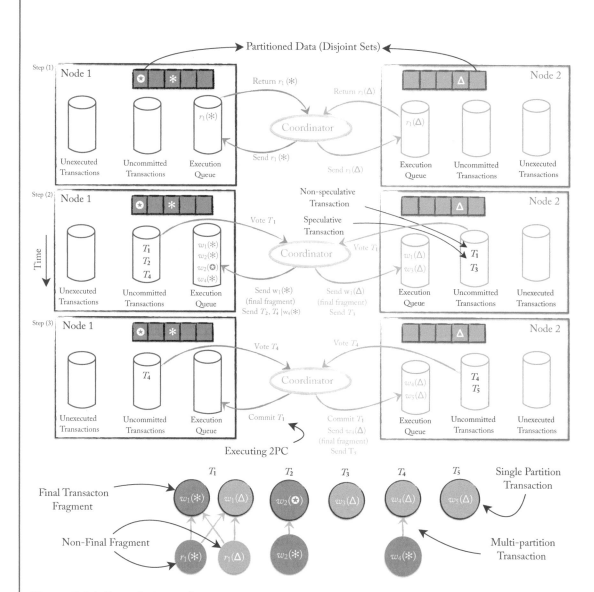

Figure 3.14: **Speculative multi-partition execution.**

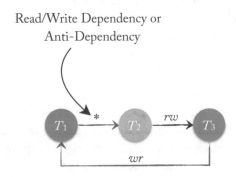

Figure 3.15: BCC (balanced concurrency control) to reduce false aborts: an essential unserializable pattern.

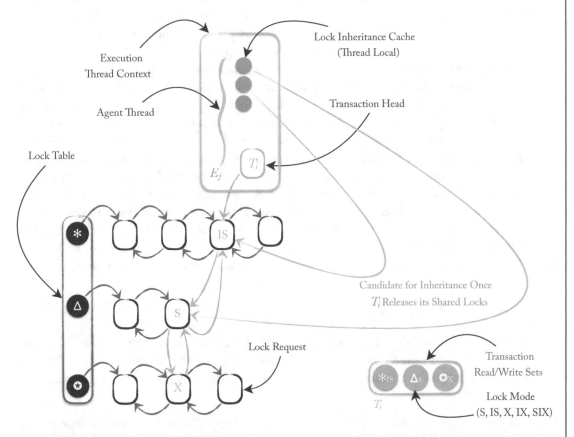

Figure 3.16: Speculative lock inheritance (SLI).

cal locking schemes in which the coarse-grained intent locks (e.g., table-level) are continuously being acquired and released by every single transaction while most transactions are expected to access only a handful of rows, thus, rarely these high-level locks are acquired in exclusive modes.

3.2.2   ORTHRUS

Ren et al. [107] propose ORTHRUS, a database prototype based on the separation of concerns and data partitioning principles. Similar to DORA [99], it offers a new threading model driven based on the database functionality as opposed to assigning a transaction to a single thread responsible for all aspects, e.g., concurrency, data access, index probing, and logging. ORTHRUS distinguishes the concurrency control and transaction logic components, and each is assigned its own dedicated thread pool, referred to as concurrency threads and execution threads, respectively, as illustrated in Figure 3.17. Furthermore, ORTHRUS adopts the partitioning model of DORA by partitioning the lock manager (instead of partitioning the primary indexes employed by DORA) to increase both data and instruction cache locality. Each data partition is assigned a unique concurrency thread responsible for granting and releasing locks for this partition. The concurrency thread follows a consumer-producer communication model that is based on queues.

On the other hand, the execution threads are responsible for all aspects of transaction logic including data access, except for interacting with the lock manager. The execution thread simply places all lock requests into the lock manger's queues based on the data partition that is being accessed. In order to avoid deadlocks, similar to Calvin, ORTHRUS assumes the read/write set of the transactions are known in advance [129],[4] and all locks are acquired in some predetermined order and execution is delayed until all locks are acquired in order to avoid deadlocks. To further optimize concurrency and execution threads and avoid multiple rounds of communications, based on the predetermined lock order, the execution thread identifies its highest priority lock to be acquired first and sends all its lock requests to the concurrency thread responsible for its highest priority lock. All remaining locks are acquired on behalf of the execution thread in the well-defined order by the concurrency thread. If the concurrency thread is not responsible for a particular data item, then the lock request is forwarded to the appropriate thread, as shown in Figure 3.17.

3.2.3   VLL: VERY LIGHTWEIGHT LOCKING

Ken et al. [108] introduced very lightweight locking (VLL) technique to reduce the lock manager overhead needed to orchestrate most pessimistic concurrency control protocols. The key idea is to decentralize the locking data structure from the central lock manager to incorporat-

---

[4]If the read/write sets are not known, then Calvin suggested a "reconnaissance" technique, in which the transaction logic is executed in passive mode in order to determine the read/write sets without acquiring any locks or making any changes to the data [129]. Once read/write sets are populated, the transaction is then ran in a normal mode. This is an optimistic, best-effort approach as the gathered read/write set can be changed once the transaction resumes the normal mode, in which case the transaction would be aborted and restarted.

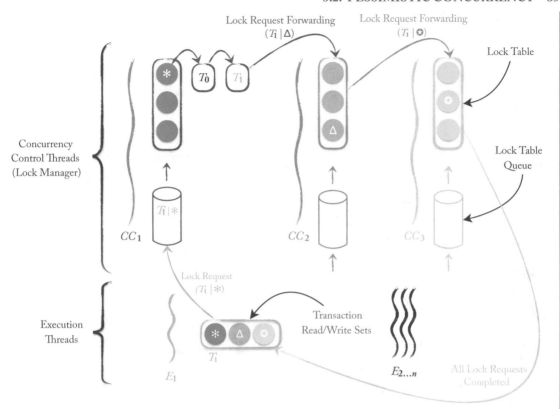

Figure 3.17: **ORTHRUS** partitioned functionality and lock planning.

ing the row-level locks as meta-data attached to each memory-resident record individually,[5] as demonstrated in Figure 3.18. Storing the lock info along the record contiguously may further improve the cache locality of in-memory stores. Furthermore, VLL stores shared and exclusive counter (C_s & C_x, respectively) for outstanding requests instead of maintaining a linked list of requests.

In 2VCC [112], only read counters were maintained which eliminates the need for write counters. Transactions in VLL abort when encountering write-write conflicts. VLL explicitly tracks write requests, yet it does not store who the lock requester is. This introduces a new challenge to resolve lock inheritance while avoiding starvation. To tackle the inheritance challenge, VLL assumes knowing the transaction read/write set as *a prior* and proposes requesting all locks at once, in a sense establishing a global order determined by the order in which transactions request their locks. The VLL design further advocates for the partitioned model of H-

---

[5]The idea of decentralizing locking also manifested in the indirection technique proposed in [110–112, 115, 116] where the indirection mapping would hold read counters which could be stored either in a separate data structure or as a column of a table.

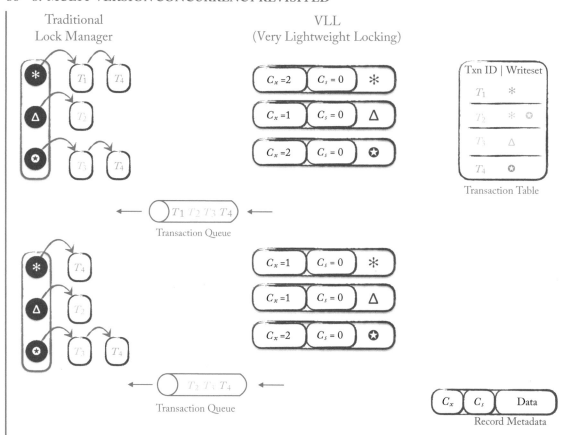

Figure 3.18: **Very lightweight locking (VLL) architecture.**

Store [57], Thus, transaction ordering among all partitions must be consistent in the presence of multi-partition transactions. This partition coordination could be eliminated by resorting to a deterministic serial order of transactions on which all partitions have agreed upon.

When a transaction completes and releases its locks, then VLL needs to walk the list of all blocked transactions, due to lock conflicts, sorted in the global order to identify the next transaction that is safe to execute, for which all of its locks are granted. To accelerate identifying the next safe transaction, VLL introduces selective contention analysis (SCA) [108] that simulates the traditional lock manager using Bloom filters to keep track of all locks held in a lossy manner. When a transaction requests shared or exclusive locks on the record Δ and $*$, it flags the lock as taken in the corresponding shared and exclusive Bloom filter, $D_S[h(\Delta)] = 1$ and $D_X[h(*)] = 1$, respectively, as illustrated in Figure 3.19. To determine if a transaction is safe then there must be no conflict among the read-write set of the transaction and all the lock

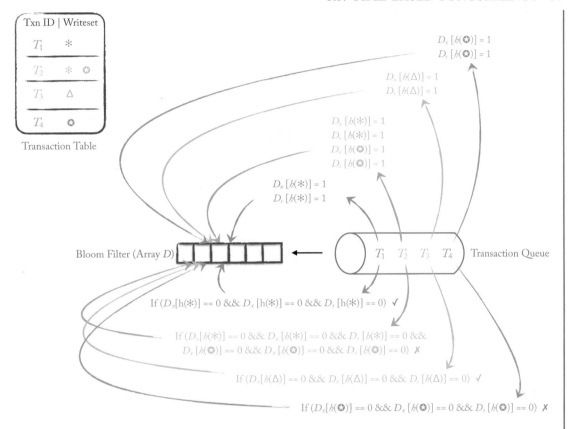

Figure 3.19: VLL's selective contention analysis (identifying non-conflicting transactions).

requests flagged in the Bloom filters, i.e., $D_X[h(readset)] == 0$, $D_X[h(writeset)] == 0$, and $D_S[h(writeset)] == 0$.

3.3   TIME-BASED CONCURRENCY

3.3.1   TICTOC

Yu et al. [146] introduced a new time-ordering optimistic concurrency protocol that tracks read/write timestamps for each record and lazily computes a valid transaction commit time based on the transaction read/write set and without the need for centralized timestamp allocation. As illustrated in Figure 3.20, the commit time of transaction T_i is logically induced and bounded to a valid time range such that: (1) readsets of conflicting concurrent transactions are not invalidated and overwritten by T_i, satisfying the read repeatability condition; (2) uncommitted writes of concurrent transactions destined to commit after T_i remain invisible, satisfying the read visibility condition and enforcing a non-conflicting serial ordering of transactions; and (3) the valid

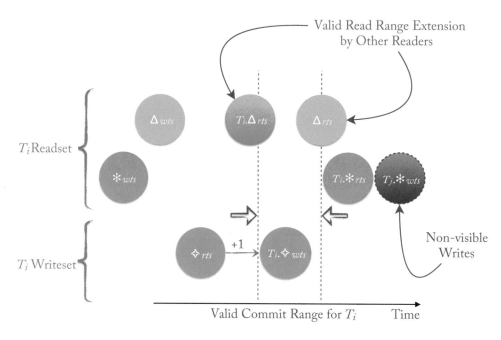

Figure 3.20: TicToc lazy commit time computation.

commit range of T_i is extended up to the last read timestamp of the records in T_i's readset, the last read may be executed by any concurrent transaction.

Another key aspect of the TicToc protocol is the validation phase, in which all records in the transaction writeset must be locked first (reminiscent of the 2VCC certification phase [112]), before lazily computing the transaction commit time. Since all writes are known at commit time, all locks are acquired in predetermined ordered to avoid deadlocks [146].

3.3.2   PSI: POSTERIOR SNAPSHOT ISOLATION

Zhou et al. [149] focused on eliminating the need for centralized timestamp allocation, which they identified as the main bottleneck on a highly parallel architecture. They introduce posterior snapshot isolation (PSI), enabling each transaction to determine its commit time autonomously. The key idea is to delay the timestamp assignment and induce a logical time. The basic snapshot isolation semantics must satisfy two conditions: (1) *consistent snapshot*: all writes committed before T_i's start time are visible and any writes after the start time are invisible; and (2) *total update order*: update transactions must commit in a total order, namely, if two concurrent transactions attempt to modify the same data item only one will succeed. PSI breaks down the consistency criterion further as (i) *atomic visibility*: no partial visibility is possible, either all or none of the updates of T_j is visible to T_i; and (ii) *temporal ordering*: all transactions committed prior to the start of t_i are visible. PSI must satisfy *atomic visibility*, *temporal ordering*, and *total update order* criteria.

The key insight is to introduce a weaker consistency model referred to as Consistent Visibility (CV) that requires *atomic visibility*, i.e., identifying concurrent conflicting transactions by tracking data dependencies, and a total update order. CV is not concerned with the *temporal ordering* that identifies the set of visible transactions, which ultimately requires placing the transactions on an induced logical timeline; hence, no notion of time is needed. The total order of writes is achieved by acquiring write locks and releasing them upon commit. Put differently, a CV scheduler (as shown in Figure 3.21) can satisfy atomic visibility by tracking the anti-dependency as follows:

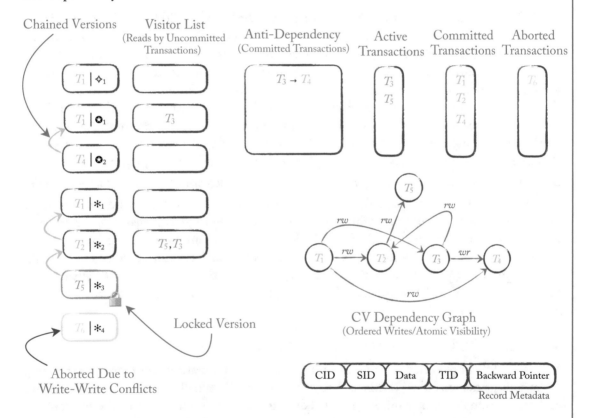

Figure 3.21: Consistency visibility (CV) in posterior snapshot isolation (PostSI).

1. The transaction T_i always reads the latest committed version of the record that is visible, and T_i adds itself to the visitor list of the visible version. A data item is visible if there is no anti-dependency on the writer of the record. For example, T_3 must read $\odot_1$ written by T_1 because $\odot_2$ was written by T_4, and there exists the anti-dependency $T_3 \xrightarrow{wr} T_4$; thus,

all writes by T_4 must be invisible to T_3. Once the visible version is identified, T_3 is added to the visitor list of ✪$_1$.

2. When a transaction T_i writes a data item (only after the write lock is granted), the latest version of the record must be visible, namely, no outstanding anti-dependency on the writer of the latest version. For example, ✱$_2$ is the latest committed version of the record written by T_2 that is visible to T_5 as there are no anti-dependency $T_5 \xrightarrow{wr} T_2$. Thus, the write lock is granted and the write is completed. Once T_5 commits, since there is an outstanding reader T_3 on the version updated by T_5, then $T_3 \xrightarrow{wr} T_5$ is added to the anti-dependency table to ensure that no writes of T_5 are visible to T_3.

A CV schedule can be transformed into a PSI schedule if a valid time interval is assigned to each transaction in order to satisfy the *temporal ordering* condition. To avoid centralized timestamp allocation and coordination, each transaction maintains an upper and a lower bound for its start and commit times. As the transaction progresses, these bounds are adjusted to satisfy the visibility criteria. At commit time, if there is a valid start and commit time within this bound then the transaction can proceed, otherwise it will be aborted. Similar to TicToc [146], read and write timestamps for each version of the record are maintained. The read timestamp holds the maximum start time of the reader and write timestamp holds the commit time of the writer. When the transaction T_j read the latest visible version written by T_i, i.e., implying the dependency $T_i \xrightarrow{rw} T_j$, then the lower bound of T_j's start time is increased to be at least as large as T_i's commit time. At commit time, if there is an anti-dependency $T_i \xrightarrow{rw} T_j$, depending whether T_i or T_j commit first, we raise the commit lower bound of T_i to be greater than T_j's start time or lower the start of the upper bound of T_j to be lower than T_i's commit time, respectively.

Unlike the serializability schedule that enforces a total ordering among transactions, namely, given any pair of transactions either T_i is visible to T_j ($c_i < c_j$) or T_j is visible T_i ($c_j < c_i$), both CV and PSI permit schedules such that there may be two concurrent transactions that are mutually invisible to one another.

3.3.3 RANGE CONFLICT MANAGEMENT

Lomet et al. [81] proposed a new multi-version concurrency control that employs timestamp range management to reduce conflicts. A timestamp range is defined as a valid commit bound for each transaction that is dynamically adjusted during the execution to reflect read/write conflicts with concurrent transactions. Notably, dynamically adjusting the commit bound inspired later works such as TicToc [146] and PSI [149] that were discussed earlier. The key idea of the proposed timestamping conflict manager (TCM) is to balance when a transaction must block. For example: (1) when the last committed version of the record is not visible to the reader, then instead of aborting, the reader is blocked until the writer commits; and (2) when positioning the reader before the writer is possible, then the reader is allowed to proceed while the writer commit is delayed. These decisions formalized as temporal constraints form the basis to dynamically adjust the commit bound of each transaction, as captured in Figure 3.22. Therefore, TCM does resemble the traditional lock manager when it comes to detecting conflicts, but it offers a more flexible conflict resolution by re-ordering transactions through adjusting their commit times whenever possible.

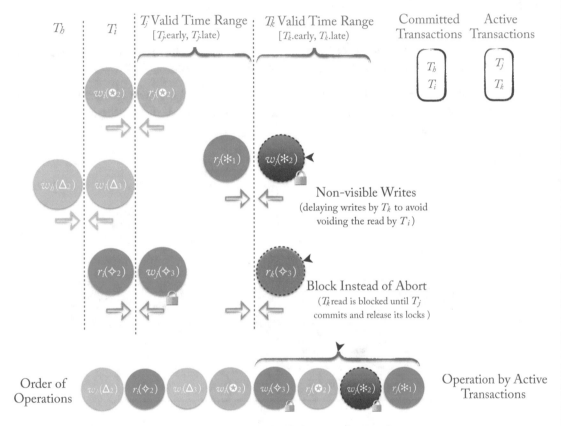

Figure 3.22: Adjusting transaction timestamp valid range for conflict operations.

3.3.4   SSN: SERIAL SAFETY NET

Wang et al. [133] introduced a serializability-enforcing certifier, referred to as a serial safety net (SSN), that can be incorporated on top of selected concurrency control protocols[6] that support a weaker isolation semantics, e.g., read committed or snapshot isolation. SSN can transform these weaker protocols to offer stronger serializable semantics by avoiding anomalies such as a write skew. The core idea is to track transactional dependencies and abort transactions that may result in a cycle in the dependency graph. In the same spirit as [81, 146, 149], SSN maintains a valid

---

[6]Any supported protocols must at least prevent lost writes and dirty reads.

commit range, referred to as the exclusion window, in which a transaction can safely commit without introducing any dependency cycle.

SSN maintains a directed graph $\mathcal{G}$ that holds the dependencies among all committed transactions, where vertices are the committed transactions and edges are serialization dependencies. For each uncommitted transaction T_i, its exclusion window $[\pi(T_i), \eta(T_i)]$ must satisfy the following constraints (as shown in Figure 3.23):

1. $\pi(T_i)$ must be equal to or larger than the commit times of all forward edges in $\mathcal{G}$, which signifies that T_i's conflicting predecessor committed first; and

2. $\eta(T_i)$ must be equal or larger than the commit times of all backward edges in $\mathcal{G}$, which signifies that T_i's conflicting successor committed first, hence the successor dependency can only be and anti-dependency.

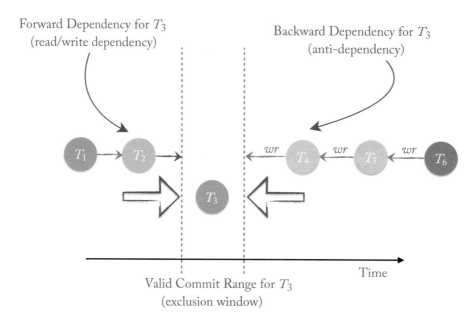

Figure 3.23: The SSN serializability-enforcing certifier detects a cycle within an exclusion window.

3.4   MULTI-VERSION STORAGE MODEL

3.4.1   LSA: LINEAGE-BASED STORAGE ARCHITECTURE

Sadoghi et al. [110, 111] introduced the lineage-based storage architecture (LSA), an update-friendly, data-model agnostic model designed to bridge the gap between transactional and analytical workloads within operational multi-version data stores. The abstract idea of LSA consists of two key ideas: (i) physical update independence by de-coupling data and its updates and (ii) lazy snapshot reconstruction via in-page lineage tracking and lineage mapping, as demonstrated in Figure 3.24. The base data is kept in read-only data blocks, where a block is simply an ordered set of objects of any type, while the modifications to the data blocks are accumulated in the corresponding lineage blocks. A lineage mapping sits in between, akin to the indirection mapping [115, 116] that links an object in data blocks to its recent updates in a lineage block, thereby decoupling updates from the physical location of objects. Each object in the base data is assigned a stable reference, i.e., an *anchored RID*, that is permanent and never changes. In contrast, the updates (or the delta) are assigned a strictly monotonically increasing reference. Therefore, both the base and the updated data are retrievable from the lineage mapping.

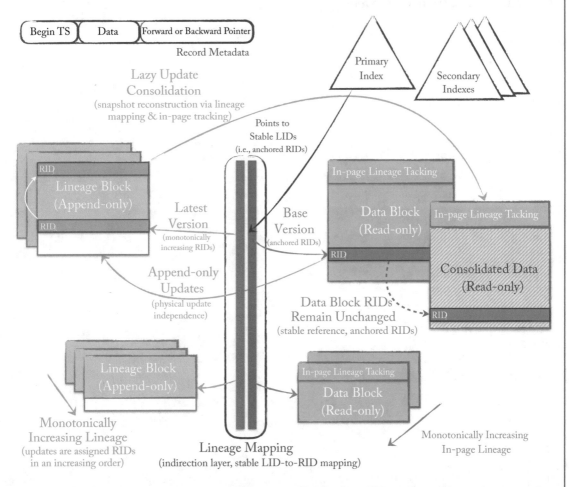

Figure 3.24: Lineage-based storage architecture (LSA; physical update independence by de-coupling data and its updates through lineage mapping).

Through a lazy background process, recent updates are merged with their corresponding read-only base data in order to construct a new set of consolidated data blocks (necessary to ensure high analytical query performance). Furthermore, each data block tracks its lineage in-page, i.e., maintains the lineage of the update history consolidated thus far. The lineage tracks how many committed updates have been applied so far to a data block; recall that update receives monotonically increasing RIDs, thus, by design, the lineage is also monotonically increasing.

By exploiting decoupling and in-page lineage tracking, the write paths of update queries and the merge process are disjoint to produce a highly scalable distributed storage layer that is updatable. The merge process only creates a new set of read-only consolidated data blocks and proceeds completely independently from update queries, which only append changes to lineage blocks and update the lineage mapping.

CHAPTER 4

Coordination-Avoidance Concurrency

The previous chapter focused on transaction processing schemes that attempt to non-deterministically identify the most effective interleaving of transaction operations. Such non-determinism is not a fundamental necessity as it often results in high abort rates and transaction restarts for contention-intensive workloads. This has led to a new wave of deterministic transaction processing, e.g., [37, 103, 129, 144] that primarily attempts to remove any non-deterministic code path from the transaction execution logic, thereby, eliminating all execution-induced aborts, e.g., due to deadlocks in the pessimistic arena or failed validation in its optimistic counterpart. Of course, logic-induced aborts are still possible for deterministic transactions, e.g., withdrawing money when the account balance does not have sufficient funds.

4.1 RESTRICTIVE CONCURRENCY

4.1.1 H-STORE

One of the first systems that questioned the status quo for concurrency control mechanisms is H-Store [57]. In H-Store, Kallman et al. [57] abandoned the need to have a complex concurrency control protocol and simply advocated to execute transactions serially in isolation on each disjoint partition of data [57]. This is only feasible if the workload is partitionable, each transaction's partition can be identified *a priori*, there exist as many partitions as the number of available compute cores, and the load is balanced across partitions. In such scenarios, without a doubt, H-Store performs exceedingly well.

This simple and effective model breaks once a transaction needs to access data on more than one partition. Multi-partition transactions become prohibitively more expensive as they require coordination across partitions, even if these partitions are assigned to different threads. To address the problem of multi-partition transactions, speculative execution and lightweight locking mechanisms have been explored [40, 48, 55, 103, 108, 128, 129] for both centralized and distributed execution.

4.1.2 CALVIN

Thomson et al. [129] proposed one of the first deterministic protocols, referred to as Calvin, that was designed to reduce the cost of two-phase commit (i.e., the agreement protocol) for distributed transactions. Incoming transactions are batched and sequenced by assigning a serial order among them. Once an agreed upon order is established among sequencers, all the concurrent executions downstream are performed deterministically for each node participating in a multi-partition transaction. Furthermore, the same serial order is applied to all replicas simultaneously.

To satisfy the pre-determined order of transactions, the read/write sets are also assumed to be known *a priori* and all locks required by a transaction are acquired before the start of the transaction based on a consistent global order (e.g., in the increasing order of the accessed key). Since transactions are processed in batches, a new batch can only start upon the completion of the previous batch. Furthermore, Calvin assumes that at least one replica is always available otherwise either the entire system will be blocked or consistency may be compromised. Alternatively, if all replicas for a partition have failed, then Calvin resorts to a weaker assumption that there are no logic-induced aborts,[1] assuming no application invariants or constraints will be violated when all replicas fail. Thus, all participating nodes are able to locally commit the transaction successfully. This assumption essentially means that the consistency of the system is compromised in favor of availability, which follows the classical Consistency-Availability-Partitionability (CAP) theorem [19].

4.1.3   LADS

Yao et al. [144] proposed LADS, a deterministic transaction technique that focuses on single-threaded, deterministic concurrency by planning and resolving all transaction conflicts before the start of the execution. LADS also assumes knowing the read/write sets of the transaction and employs a graph-based approach to plan and build dependency graphs as a blueprint to guide the deterministic execution. As shown in Figure 4.1, LADS operates in four stages: (i) transaction batching, (ii) dependency graph construction, (iii) dynamic graph partitioning, and (iv) single-threaded execution.

Given a set of transaction batches, for each batch, LADS concurrently constructs a dependency graph among the transactions. These graphs are further partitioned to smaller chunks to be load balanced among executor threads. Once the graph is constructed and partitioned, each partition is processed by a single executor thread while respecting inter- and intra-graph dependencies. Therefore, to correctly process transactions across graph partitions, communication among executor threads is necessary.

4.2   DETERMINISTIC PLANNING OPTIMIZATION

4.2.1   LAZY EVALUATION

Faleiro et al. [39] introduced a notion of *lazy* transaction execution to allow communicating the commit/abort decision to the user without fully executing the transaction, a contrast to

---

[1]Recall there are no execution-induced aborts after eliminating non-determinism.

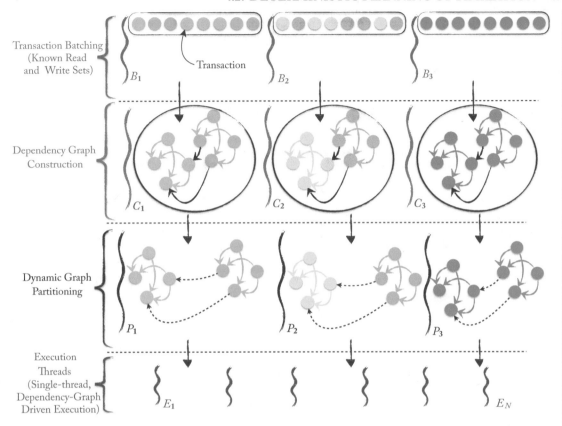

Figure 4.1: LADS single-threaded execution model.

the traditional model that demands a complete eager execution. The lazy evaluation follows the deterministic paradigm and assumes that the read/write set is known *a priori*; hence, no execution-induced abort is possible. To ensure there are no logic-induced errors, the transaction is decomposed into two phases (as shown in Figure 4.2).

1. A now-phase that includes executing any reads needed to ensure all database and application constraints are satisfied or reads needed to determine the write set. Additionally, the entire write set of the transaction must be tagged as sticky. Reading a sticky record requires substantiating its value by executing the transaction T_i that last modified the record. This may result in a chain execution of other transactions that T_i depends on.

2. A later-phase includes all write operations that were stickified in the now-phase and must be substantiated at a later point once an interested transaction arrives.

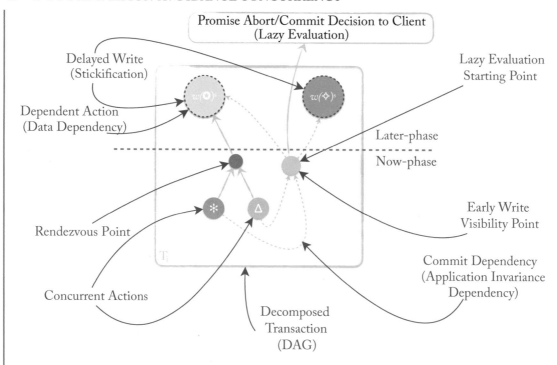

Figure 4.2: Lazy transaction evaluation: now-phase vs. later-phase.

As demonstrated in Figure 4.3, the life cycle of each version of the record undergoes two stages: stickification and substantiation. Stickification is the initial stage that marks the creation of a new version of the record r_j by simply noting there is a pending write by T_i. The substantiation stage is the actual execution of pending writes by T_i to determine the value of r_j. Substantiation may further trigger the execution of all unsubstantiated transactions on which T_i transitively depends on. During the now-phase, all transactions (substantiated or not) are logged, transaction dependencies are derived, and all writes are stickified.[2] Once a reader arrives, for example, interested in a record written by the transaction T_4 in Figure 4.3, then all the transactions that it transitively depends on are forced to execute and make their writes visible and durable by substantiating the transactions $T_1 \cdots T_3$.

4.2.2 EARLY WRITE VISIBILITY

Faleiro et al. [38] introduced the piece-wise visibility (PWV) technique centered around the notion of *early write visibility* that exploits the ability to determine the commit decision of a transaction—making its uncommitted write visible—before completing all of its operations.

---

[2]Notably, the process of stickification does result in physical writes to each record in the writeset in order to mark the responsible pending transaction.

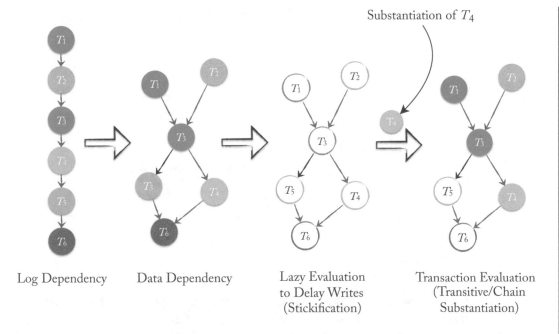

Figure 4.3: Delayed, transitive, chained substantiation.

The idea of early write visibility is the basis of lazy evaluation introduced earlier by Faleiro et al. [39] such that instead of making the writes visible eagerly, the execution of physical writes are arbitrarily delayed until a reader requests to see the latest value of a modified record (cf. Section 4.2.1). PWV's deterministic execution model is based on traversing transaction dependency graph resembling LADS [144] and assumes knowing the read/write set *a priori*. The way transactions are decomposed into a directed acycle graph (DAG) with rendezvous points follows DORA's execution model [99], as demonstrated in Figure 4.4. These abortable rendezvous points are critical points in the execution during which the application invariants can be validated (detecting if logic-induced aborts is possible). If successful, then the transaction is guaranteed to commit and writes can be made visible because all execution-induced aborts are eliminated by following a deterministic concurrency protocol [103, 144].

4.2.3   BOHM

In the same spirit of [38, 39], Faleiro et al. [37] introduced a deterministic multi-version concurrency control variant, named BOHM, that separates the concurrency control logic from the execution logic while assuming the complete *a priori* knowledge of transactions' write sets. The BOHM protocol consists of two sequential phases. The first phase is the concurrency control phase, where the transaction serialization order is determined, which includes dependency track-

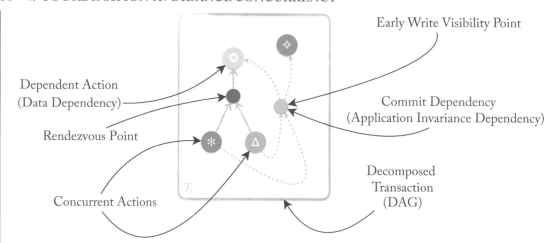

Figure 4.4: **Early write visibility.**

ing and version management. Record placeholders are installed for yet to be executed writes in this phase. The second phase is the execution phase, during which the transaction logic is applied in the serial order determined in the first phase. BOHM eliminates read/write contention: readers never block writers, while readers read from preassigned record placeholders. Thus, no locking is required to safeguard and validate the reads, but reads are delayed if the placeholder record is not initialized yet. Reads may be aborted (with a potential risk of cascading aborts) if an uncommitted record is read unless techniques such as early write visibility [38] are adopted.

CHAPTER 5

Novel Transactional System Architectures

As the hardware landscape changes, database system designers continuously seek opportunities to utilize the new resources. The current trends point to massive concurrency in a single box due to the emergence of many-core architectures coupled with the substantial increase in the size of main memory at a diminishing cost. Thus, there are a multitude of promising research avenues to reshape the storage and transaction layers of the next-generation data platforms to offer much higher transaction performance by leveraging the unprecedented level of parallelism while rethinking the traditional system architecture.

For decades, conventional wisdom has prescribed separating the management of transactional and analytical data, leading to the creation and deployment of specialized engines that are fine-tuned to each workload, which is a necessary compromise to offset technology limitations. But in the age of digitalization, the enterprise now recognizes the need of day-to-day operation based on real-time, actionable insights in order to gain a competitive edge. This implies the necessity of making real-time analytical decisions directly over transactional data—the *latest data*[1] or *fresh data*.[2]

In this chapter, we first discuss concurrency protocols that are exclusively designed for multi-core architecture before shifting our attention to the unification of the transactional and analytical capabilities.

5.1 HARDWARE-AWARE CONCURRENCY

What distinguishes the concurrency protocols in this section from the aforementioned techniques is the keen attention to multi-socket, many-core architectures and consequently the arising challenges such as the increased contention among competing cores and non-uniform memory accesses (NUMA). These challenges translate to a number of critical performance-hindering issues including blocking synchronization mechanisms or frequent aborts due to deadlocks and failed optimistic validation, as well as cache misses, cache coherency, and false sharing phenomena.

---

[1]By analytics on *latest data*, we imply the ability to run the query on any desired level of isolations such as dirty read, committed read, snapshot read, repeatable read, or serializable [42].

[2]By analytics on *fresh data*, we imply running queries on a recent snapshot that is not necessarily the latest possible snapshot or a consistent one [42].

5.1.1   DORA: DATA-ORIENTED ARCHITECTURE

Unlike the classical execution model, in which each transaction is assigned to a single thread, DORA [99] proposed a novel reformulation of transaction processing as a loosely coupled publish/subscribe paradigm. The primary goal of DORA is to improve cache efficiency using a thread-to-data assignment as opposed to the thread-to-transaction assignment, while the underlying concurrency model continues to follow classic pessimistic concurrency protocols. DORA decomposes each transaction into a set of rendezvous points (which later was employed in [38, 39]) and relies on message passing for thread communication, as demonstrated in Figure 5.1.

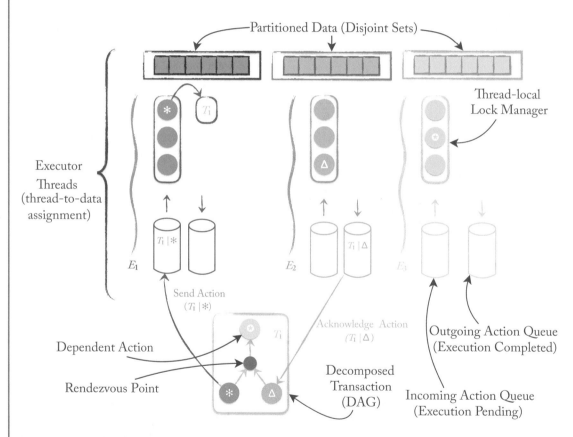

Figure 5.1: **DORA** data-oriented execution architecture.

DORA assigns a thread to a set of records based on how the primary key index is traversed, often a B-tree index, where essentially the tree divides the key space into a set of contiguous disjoint ranges, and each range is assigned to a thread. Decomposed transactions take on the role of producer of operations on records and the thread responsible for a range of records acts as a consumer, consuming the operations for the set of records it covers. Although DORA relies on a traditional lock manager, each thread maintains its local lock manager for its assigned partition (the net effect of it is similar to [107]), thereby, reducing the contention on the lock manager.

5.1.2 SILO

Tu et al. [132] introduced Silo that revolves around an optimistic concurrency variant that focuses on eliminating any centralized contention point and improving cache efficiency. Instead of maintaining a globally synchronized clock, Silo adopts a decentralized transaction identifier generation. It further avoids read side effects such as acquiring locks or maintaining read counters or the last read timestamp, all of which force a read operation to write in the shared memory and lead to potential cache invalidation and cache coherency protocol invocation. Silo's architecture, unlike H-Store [57], assumes that the workloads is non-partitionable. Its execution timeline is sliced and committed at epoch units consisting of a batch of transactions. Within each epoch, Silo strictly relies on record-level redo logging. At the heart of Silo's protocol, every thread maintains only a loosely synchronized clock to eliminate the need for central coordination while supporting serializable isolation semantics. Simply put, the key realization is that one can maintain only a total write order per record within an epoch, for which a loosely synchronized clock is sufficient, as opposed to maintaining a total order per transaction which may require a synchronized global clock. The overall architecture of Silo is captured in Figure 5.2.

In Silo, the global timestamp allocation is based on a coarse-grained interval, referred to as an epoch. Within each epoch, transactions are assigned unique transaction identifiers (TIDs), analogous to a timestamp, serving as their commit counter. TIDs are generated from a combination of the monotonically increasing global epoch counter plus the local thread counter, therefore, the relative order of transactions across threads is lost. Put differently, the thread local clocks are loosely synchronized at a coarse-grained epoch level.

Silo's basic concurrency protocol consists of three phases: an optimistic read phase, a validation phase, and a write-commit phase. The phases are outlined in Figure 5.3. Once a transaction completes its reads and locally buffers its writes, it enters the validation phase, in which the entire write set is locked in a predetermined global order; the global epoch counter is read only but it is not advanced—a coarse-grained synchronization across threads—and reads are validated to ensure that no concurrent writers invalidated them. If either write locks cannot be acquired or read validation fails, the transaction is aborted. If successful, the transaction enters the write-commit phase, in which a TID is generated within the current epoch such that it is greater than the TIDs of all the records in the read/write sets of the transaction; writes are installed with the assigned TID; and at the end of epoch, the record-level redo logs are flushed, and the group commit is completed. Log replay applies record-level redo actions and strictly follows the TID order in the log, which establishes a total order on writes.

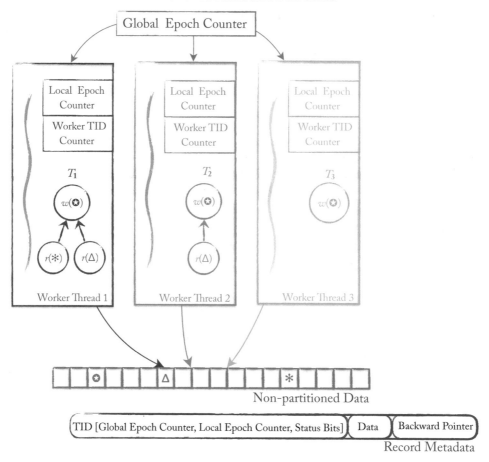

Figure 5.2: The Silo non-partitioned data store.

Due to how transaction identifiers (TIDs) are generated, the read-after-write dependency is satisfied because the commit time of the transaction must be greater than the TID of records that are accessed. However, the write-after-read anti-dependencies are not reflected in TID generation (although reads are validated) because the relative ordering of transactions is not maintained. Serializable execution is possible, but transactions across threads must be committed and logged as a unit in the same epoch. Partial epoch commit or recovery that requires total ordering of individual transaction is not possible, i.e., the serial order within the epoch is not recoverable from the log. The log is strictly a record-level redo-logging (operational logging is not possible). As a result, within a committed epoch, a record-level serial ordering is only recoverable that is dictated by TIDs and recovering the transaction serial orders is not possible because they are not reflected in TID generation. Furthermore, due to the lack of relative ordering, supporting

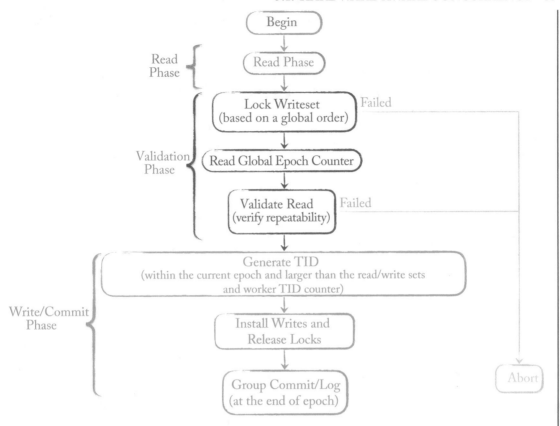

Figure 5.3: The Silo epoch-based optimistic concurrency control protocol uses a decentralized transaction identifier generation technique.

weaker isolation semantics is non-trivial and forming an arbitrary consistent snapshot of data is not possible; hence, isolation semantics such as snapshot read or snapshot isolation are not supported.

5.1.3 FOEDUS: FAST OPTIMISTIC ENGINE FOR DATA UNIFICATION SERVICES

Kimura [64] introduced FOEDUS, an open-source database engine that revolves around a novel storage architecture based on dual-page and stratified snapshot designs, as demonstrated in Figure 5.4. The key idea of the dual-page design is to maintain a physically independent but logically equivalent dual of every updated page, namely, a mutable, volatile page in DRAM along with its immutable, nonvolatile dual page in NVRAM. Every time a page gets updated, a mutable version of that page is constructed (if it does not exist already) in the main memory through the copy-on-write technique. All changes by transactions are applied to the volatile pages, keeping their non-volatile dual pages intact. Periodically, new snapshot pages are constructed from the stable committed transaction log that entail the latest modifications, which essentially creates a new immutable page by merging the latest changes to the last snapshot page and eliminates the need to have an immutable page until there is a new update. The final step of merging is dropping the pointers to volatile pages, at which point ongoing transactions must be drained and new transactions FOEDUS must be delayed temporarily, a central contention point that was eliminated in LSA design [111].

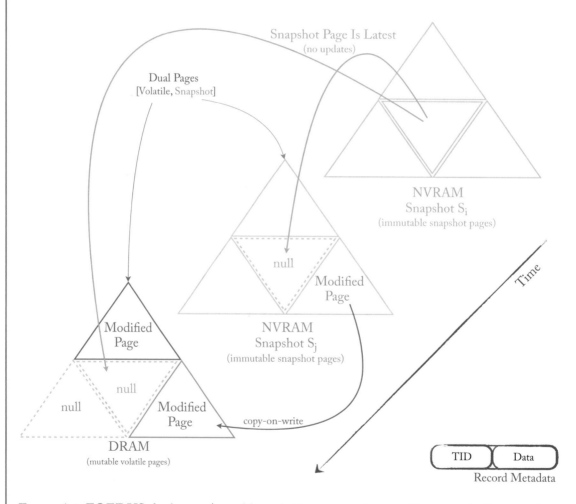

Figure 5.4: **FOEDUS** dual page (mutable, volatile page vs. immutable, nonvolatile, snapshot page) storage architecture based on a stratified snapshot design.

Older snapshot pages are further maintained in a hierarchical or stratified fashion. The merge process essentially enables quick and durable access to the latest committed version of data, a reminiscent LSM-Tree in [96]. But unlike LSM-Tree, in both FOEDUS [64] and LSA [111], the latest version of the record can be fetched by examining one layer without the need for searching the entire hierarchy or incurring the cost of maintaining a Bloom filter to skip un-related layers. The novel common ground between FOEDUS and LSA is the notion of physical update independence (cf. Section 3.4.1) that decouples data and its updates, which manifested as dual pages [64] or lineage mapping [111], respectively. FOEDUS further keeps identical page boundaries (i.e., a range of keys) for both the mutable and the immutable pages, which in general does introduce additional complexities when page sizes change after modifying the content of a page or when snapshot pages are compressed to optimize analytical queries while the mutable pages are uncompressed. Going one step further, LSA's design eliminated the need for maintaining identical page boundarie and adopted a generic update design by strictly relying on an append-only (instead of in-place update mechanism used in FOEDUS) mechanism when incorporating the latest changes to the mutable pages, further reducing contention of managing mutable pages.

5.1.4   MOCC: MOSTLY OPTIMISTIC CONCURRENCY

Wang et al. [134] introduced the mostly optimistic concurrency (MOCC) protocol that seeks the right balance between pessimism and optimism. MOCC breaks two-phase locking in which releasing and reacquiring lock is forbidden when serializability is desired. Serializability in MOCC is achieved by always running the validation, similar to optimistic protocol, before transitioning to the commit phase. The basis of MOCC is Silo's optimistic protocol [132], which is extended by collecting statistics about record popularity from access methods or by tracking aborted transactions. MOCC proactively locks records in shared or exclusive mode only if the record is deemed hot or when the transaction is being retried, thus introducing pessimism in the otherwise optimistic read phase of Silo.

To avoid deadlocks, MOCC strictly follows a consistent global order when requesting locks. Acquiring locks in a predetermined order during the validation phase is trivial because the complete read and write sets of the transaction are known already. However, when locks are acquired during the pre-validation phase, then a transaction may encounter locks in an order that is not aligned with a globally consistent order. To address this challenge, when a transaction is faced with an out-of-order lock request, it simply drops any locks it already holds that violate the ordering before acquiring the new lock. Again, dropping locks is correct because transactions will always be validated at a later phase: the sole purpose of pessimistic locking is to reduce the abort rate and not to enforce serializability. Therefore, at any stage, MOCC can guarantee that no new locks are ever acquired out-of-order, hence, there is no deadlock. The MOCC protocol is summarized in Figure 5.5.

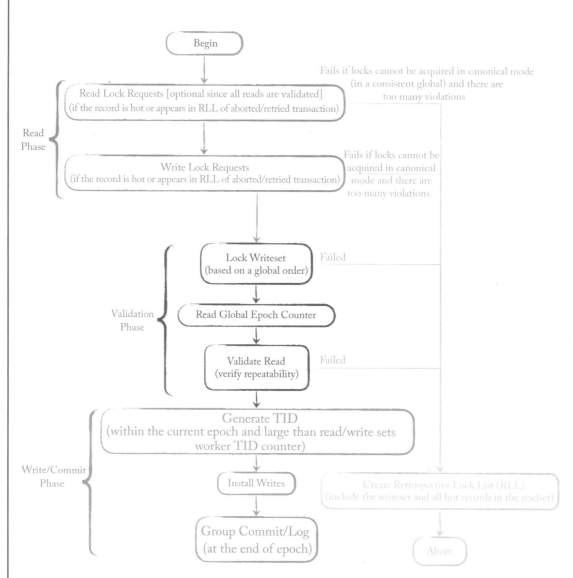

Figure 5.5: Mostly optimistic concurrency control (MOCC) using a selective, best-effort locking of hot records or the records of previously aborted/retried transactions.

5.1.5   ACC: ADAPTIVE CONCURRENCY CONTROL

Tang et al. [126] presented a framework to adaptively support a variety of concurrency protocols (e.g., optimistic, pessimistic, or single-threaded execution model) while dynamically clustering data and choosing the optimal concurrency protocols within each cluster. This work is motivated by the observation that a single concurrency protocol may be unable to cope with dynamic shifts in diverse workloads. As demonstrated in Figure 5.6, the authors present an adaptive concurrency control (ACC) framework that highlights key challenges: (1) how to partition data while minimizing cross-partition transactions; (2) how to select the most suitable concurrency protocol within each partition given its workload profile; (3) how to orchestrate the co-existence of a mixed set of concurrency schemes; and (4) how to transition from one concurrency scheme to another while ensuring transactional correctness or how to merge partitions.

In particular, ACC exploits the single-threaded execution model for partitionable workloads and when the degree of cross-partition transactions surpasses a certain threshold it merges the partitions to eliminate cross-partition coordination. Of course, there is a limit on how many partitions can be merged because all the data in the resulting partition will be served by a single thread. Thus, when multi-partition transactions cannot be eliminated, then for the low-contention partition ACC employs a no-wait two-phase locking method inspired by VLL [108], and for the high-contention partition ACC relies on an optimistic concurrency protocol based on Silo [132].

To further simplify the co-existence of concurrency protocols, ACC proposed a data-oriented mixed concurrency control protocol in which each record is managed by exactly one protocol; thus, no coordination is required on a record basis across concurrency schemes. In the same spirit, 2VCC [112] offered a more general framework to allow each record to be modified by multiple concurrency schemes (through either optimistic and pessimistic techniques), and relied on the indirection layer as a lightweight coordination mechanism among concurrency algorithms (cf. Section 3.1.3).

5.1.6   QUECC: QUEUE-ORIENTED, CONTROL-FREE CONCURRENCY

QueCC is motivated by a simple question: *Is it possible to have concurrent execution over shared data (not limited to partitionable workloads) without having any concurrency control?* In response to this question, Qadah and Sadoghi [103] proposed a queue-oriented, control-free concurrency architecture geared toward multi-socket, many-core architectures. QueCC exhibits minimal contention during execution and imposes no coordination among transactions while offering serializable guarantees. The key intuition behind the QueCC design is to eliminate concurrency control by executing a set of batched transactions in two disjoint and deterministic phases of planning and execution, namely, decompose transactions in parallel into predetermined priority queues followed by priority-queue-oriented execution (as illustrated in Figure 5.7). In other words, QueCC imposes a deterministic plan of execution on batches of transactions driven by

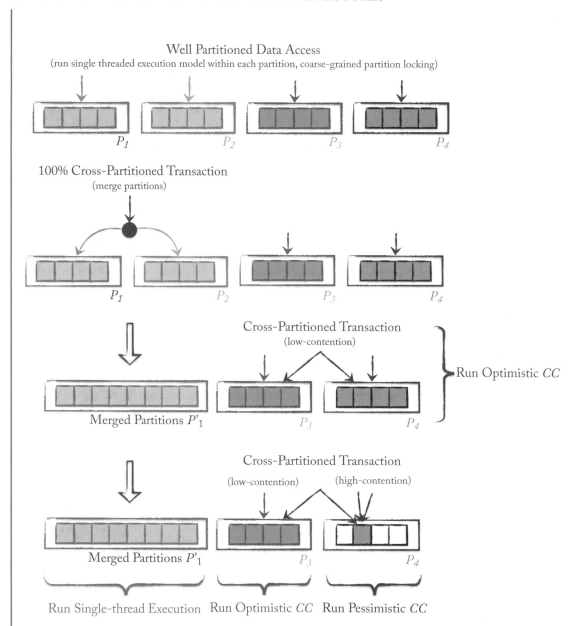

Figure 5.6: **Workload-dependent adaptive concurrency control based on single-threaded serial execution and optimistic and pessimistic protocols.**

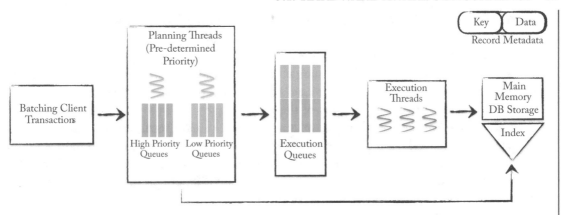

Figure 5.7: QueCC: a Queue-oriented, Control-free Concurrency architecture.

predetermined queue priority, which eliminates the need for concurrency control during the actual execution of transactions; hence, QueCC eliminates execution-induced aborts.

H-Store [57] proposed to physically partition the data into disjoint fixed sets, and under partitionable workload assumption, and each fixed partition is assigned to a thread, and within each partition, transactions are executed serially. In a sense, for each disjoint physical partition of data, a queue of transactions is created which is executed serially by a fixed thread. Unfolding the H-Store principle further, QueCC eliminates the rigidness of queues. Queues in QueCC are created dynamically for disjoint logical partitions of data and any thread can dynamically process any queue.

In QueCC, a batch of transactions is spread across planners into disjoint sets. The role of each planner is to determine the serial order locally (e.g., the incoming order), decompose the transaction into a set of read/write operations (or fragments), and place these operations into queues with respect to a serial order that is chosen locally. Each queue holds operations for a disjoint partition of data. Thus, in the planning phase, queues of operations are created over disjoint logical partitions in parallel. In the execution phase, any execution thread can begin processing any queues as long as the *execution-priority invariant* is satisfied, namely, for each record (or a queue), operations that belong to higher priority queues (created by a higher priority planner) must always be executed before executing any lower priority operations.

The detailed QueCC protocol can be described as follows. Transactions are processed in batches into two deterministic phases of planning and execution. In the planning phase, each planner receives a set of transactions for which they create prioritized execution queues without any coordination. A predetermined distinct priority is assigned to each planner thread. Priority is essential to the coordination-free design of QueCC as it allows planners to operate independently in parallel by passing on their priority to the execution queues; thus, the total ordering of transactions planned by different planner threads is preserved. The priory enables execution threads to independently decide the order of executing fragments subject to execution-priority invariance, which leads to correct serializable execution.[3]

The planner serves as a local sequencer with a predetermined priority for its assigned transactions and spreads operations of each transaction (e.g., reads and writes) into a set of queues based on the local sequence order. Each queue is defined over a disjoint set of records, and queues inherit their distinct priorities. The goal of the planner is to distribute operations into a set of almost equal-sized queues. Within each planner, queues can arbitrarily be merged or split to load balance the queues. Note that queues across planners can only be combined following the strict priority order of each planner. The execution-priority invariance is the essence of how determinism in QueCC is captured, as all planners operate at different priorities; they are planned independently and in parallel without any coordination.

Any execution thread can arbitrarily process any remaining queues without any coordination as long as the execution-priority invariance is held. Depending on how queues are dynamically defined, independent operations from the same transaction may be processed in parallel by multiple execution threads without any synchronization among the executors; this exploits both inter- and intra-transaction parallelism. Once all queues are processed, the batch is complete and all transactions are committed except those that violated any application and database-imposed constraints that cause logic-induced aborts. To ensure durability and recoverability, all parameters that are required to recreate the execution queues are logged.

5.2 HTAP: HYBRID TRANSACTIONAL AND ANALYTICAL PROCESSING

There has been a recent surge in various initiatives from both academia and industry to combine the transactional and analytical capabilities into a single Hybrid Transactional and Analytical (HTAP) system. Among existing HTAP solutions, we adopt the following classification proposed in [42]:

1. operating on a single data representation (e.g., row or column format) vs. multiple representations of data; and

2. operating on a single copy of data (i.e., single replica) vs. maintaining multiple copies of data replica.

In recent years, we have witnessed the development of many in-memory engines optimized for OLTP (online transactional processing) workloads either as research prototypes such as HyPer [61, 95], ES2 [20], and L-Store [110] (and its newer manifestation in ExpoDB [48]) or for commercial use such as Microsoft Hekaton [28], Oracle In-Memory [70], VoltDB [125],

---

[3]Weaker consistency models and weaker isolation levels can be realized in QueCC by relaxing the execution-priority invariance. For example, for the committed read isolation level, within a batch, all reads can be pushed ahead of writes irrespective of queue priority or transaction order.

and HANA [67, 101]. Most of these systems are designed to keep the data in row format and in the main memory to increase the OLTP performance. In contrast, to optimize the OLAP workloads, the columnar format is preferred. The early examples of these engines are C-Store [124] and MonetDB [18]. Major big data vendors also started integrating columnar storage formats into their existing engines. SAP HANA [40] is designed to handle both OLTP and OLAP workloads by supporting the in-memory columnar format. IBM DB2 BLU [105] introduces a novel columnar OLAP engine that is memory-optimized and substantially improves the execution of complex analytical workloads by operating directly on compressed data. In what follows, we shift our focus to the recent developments that aim to bring both OLTP and OLAP capabilities into the same platform.

HyPer, a powerful main-memory system, guarantees the ACID properties of OLTP transactions and supports running OLAP queries on consistent snapshot [61]. The design of HyPer leverages a novel OS-controlled lazy copy-on-write mechanism to create a consistent virtual memory snapshot. HyPer resorts to running transactions serially when the workload is not partitionable. Notably, HyPer employs multi-version concurrency to close this gap [95]. IBM Wildfire is a variant of DB2 BLU [105] that is integrated into Apache Spark to support fast ingestion by adopting the relaxed last-writer-wins semantics and offers an efficient snapshot isolation on recent, but stale, data by relying on periodic shipment and writing of the logs onto a distributed file system [10]. The elastic, power-aware, data-intensive cloud computing platform (epiC) was designed to provide scalable big data services on the Cloud [20]. epiC is designed to handle both OLTP and OLAP workloads [23]. The OLTP queries in ES2 are limited to basic get, put, and delete requests, and there is no support for multi-statement transactions. Furthermore, in ES2 it is possible that snapshot consistency is violated and the user is notified subsequently [20].

Microsoft SQL Server currently consists of three unique engines: (1) the classical SQL Server engine designed to process disk-based tables in row format; (2) the Apollo engine designed to maintain the data in the columnar format that offers significant performance gain for OLAP workloads [72]; and (3) the completely redesigned Hekaton in-memory engine designed to excel at OLTP workloads [28, 71]. Noteworthy, Microsoft has also recently announced moving toward supporting real-time OLTP and OLAP capabilities [71], which further reinforces the position to support real-time analytics. To support OLTP and OLAP among loosely integrated engines, an intricate foreground routine is proposed to enable a continuous data migration from Hekaton (a row-based engine) into Apollo (a columnar engine) [71].

Oracle offers a novel dual-format option to support real-time OLTP and OLAP, where data resides in both columnar and row formats [70]. To avoid maintaining two identical copies of data in both columnar and row format, an effective "layout transparency" abstraction was introduced that maps data into a set of disjoint tiles (driven by the query workload and the age of data), where a tile could be stored in either columnar or row format [7]. The key advantage of the layout-transparent mapping is that the query execution operates on the abstract representation (layout independent) without the need to create two different sets of operators for processing the column- and row-oriented data. In the same spirit, SnappyData proposed a unified runtime engine to combine streaming, transaction, and analytical processing, but from the storage perspective, it maintains recent transactional data in row format while it ages data to a columnar format for analytical processing [106]. SnappyData employs data aging strategies similar to the original version of SAP HANA [123].

5.2.1   L-STORE: LINEAGE-BASED DATA STORE

Sadoghi et al. [110, 111] introduced L-Store (Lineage-based Data Store) that combines the real-time processing of transactional and analytical workloads within a single unified engine. L-Store bridges the gap between managing data that is being updated at a high velocity and analyzing a large volume of data by introducing a novel update-friendly LSA that was briefly discussed in Section 3.1 [110–112, 115, 116]. This is achieved by developing a contention-free and lazy staging of data from write optimized into read optimized form in a transactionally consistent manner without the need to replicate data, to maintain multiple representations of data, to limit to only *fresh data* and loss of access to the *latest data*, or to develop multiple loosely integrated engines that limits real-time capabilities.

L-Store strictly keeps only one copy and one representation of data; thus, L-Store eliminates the need to maintain layout-independent mapping abstraction and storing data in both columnar and row formats. For example, HANA [67, 101] also strives to achieve real-time OLTP and OLAP engine. Most notably, both L-Store and HANA share the same philosophy that aims to develop a generalized solution for unifying OLTP and OLAP as opposed to building specialized engines. But what distinguishes L-Store's architecture from HANA is its unified columnar storage without the need to distinguish between the main store and a delta store. L-Store further proposes a contention-free merge process, whereas in [67], the merge process requires draining all active transactions at the boundary of the merge process, a contention that may result in a noticeable slowdown [110, 111].

To address the dilemma between write- and read-optimized layouts, L-Store supports a native multi-version, columnar layout (i.e., data across columns are aligned to allow implicit re-construction), where records are (virtually) partitioned into disjoint ranges (also referred to as update range), as shown in Figure 5.8. Records within each range span a set of read-only, compressed blocks, which we refer to as data blocks (cf. base pages). More importantly, for every range of records, and for each updated column within the range, L-Store maintains a set of append-only blocks to store the latest updates, which we refer to as lineage blocks (cf. tail pages). Any time a record is updated in data blocks, a new record is appended to its corresponding lineage blocks, where there are explicit values inserted only for the updated columns (non-updated columns are preassigned a special null value). The records in data blocks are referred to as the base records and the records in lineage blocks are referred to as the tail records.

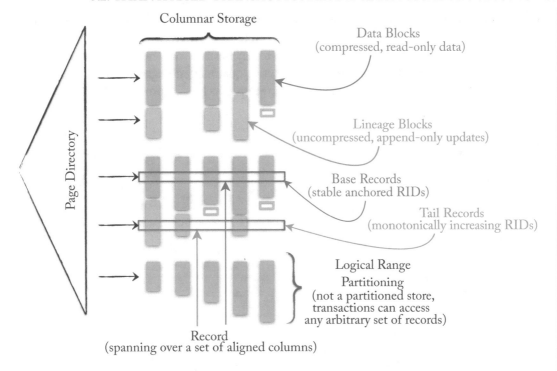

Figure 5.8: The L-Store data model.

A unique feature of the L-Store is that lineage blocks are strictly append-only and follow a write-once policy. In other words, once a value is written to a lineage block, it will not be overwritten even if the writing transaction aborts. The append-only design, together with retaining all versions of the record, substantially simplifies low-level synchronization and recovery protocol and enables efficient realization of multi-version concurrency control. Another important property of L-Store is that all data are represented in a common unified form; there are no ad-hoc corner cases.

To speed up query processing, there is also an explicit linkage (in the form of forward and backward pointers) among records. From a base record, there is a forward pointer to the latest version of the record in lineage blocks. The different versions of the same records in lineage blocks are chained together to enable fast access to an earlier version of the record. The linkage is established by introducing a table-embedded lineage mapping (i.e., an indirection column) that stores forward pointers for base records and backward pointers for tail records (i.e., RIDs). Another aspect of L-Store is a periodic, contention-free merging of a set of data blocks with its corresponding lineage blocks (as shown in Figure 5.9a). This is performed to consolidate data blocks with the recent updates and to bring data blocks forward in time (i.e., creating a set of merged blocks). Each merged block independently maintains its lineage information, i.e., keeping track of all tail records that are consolidated onto the block thus far. By maintaining explicit in-page lineage information, the current state of each block can be determined independently, and the data block can be brought up to any desired snapshot. Outdated data blocks that fall outside the snapshot boundaries of all active queries that began prior to the merge are de-allocated using an epoch-based, contention-free approach, as captured in Figure 5.9b.

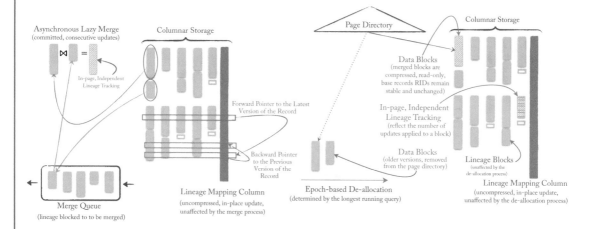

Figure 5.9: L-Store contention-free merge and de-allocation protocols.

5.2.2   EXPODB: EXPLORATORY DATA PLATFORM

The broader initiative of L-Store [110, 111] has led to the development of ExpoDB, an in-memory, distributed ledger that unifies secure transactional and real-time analytical processing, all centered around a decentralized computational model—blockchain [47, 48, 103]. Furthermore, ExpoDB serves as a testbed to study numerous concurrency, agreement, and consensus protocols. The overall architecture of ExpoDB is captured in Figure 5.10 and consists of a set of five layers.

The *Application Layer* acts as the testbed for evaluating the underlying database protocols [48] using OLTP benchmarks such as YCSB [26], TPC-C [130], and PPS [49]. The *Transport Layer* allows communication using messages between the client and server nodes. The *Execution Layer* facilitates the seamless execution of a transaction; this layer performs thread management, and implements various concurrency control protocols (e.g., QueCC [103], 2VCC [112], DORA [99], H-Store [57], Silo [132], Foedus [64], MOCC [134], Tic-Toc [146], Cicada [79]) and agreement protocols (e.g., 2PC [98], 3PC [98], Calvin [129], EasyCommit [48]). ExpoDB employs LSA for its *storage layer* [111]. Furthermore, ExpoDB extends blockchain functionality to the traditional distributed systems through a *secure layer*. To facilitate secure transactions ExpoDB provides a cryptographic variant to YCSB – *Secure YCSB*

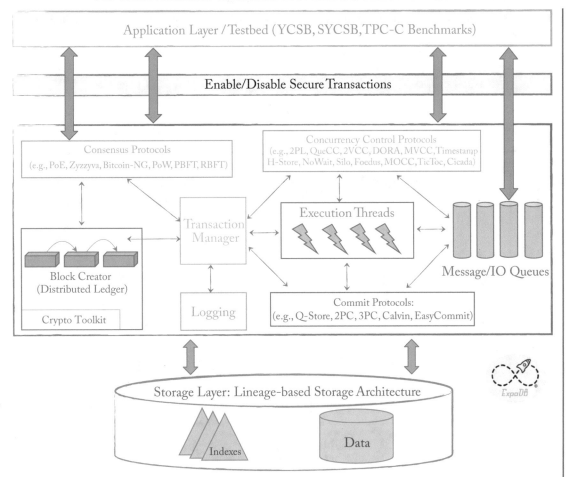

Figure 5.10: ExpoDB: a decentralized and democratic platform to unify OLTP and OLAP.

benchmark. ExpoDB also contains implementations for a variety of fault-tolerant consensus protocols such as PoW [117], Zyzzyva [66], PBFT [22], RBFT [9], and Bitcoin-NG [36].

5.2.3 BATCHDB

Makreshanski et al. [82] presented BatchDB that tackles HTAP workloads by introducing a primary-secondary replication design to efficiently isolate OLTP and OLAP workloads. BatchDB relies on batched migration of recent updates for executing OLAP queries over recent (but possibly stale) snapshots [82]. As shown in Figure 5.11, transactions are executed on the primary copy (latest data), while all analytics are executed in the secondary copy (fresh data). One key benefit of BatchDB is that it isolates the runtime environment of OLTP and OLAP, which may result in simplified scheduling and potentially better system utilization within each tightly coupled replication group. Notably, the relaxed execution model of BatchDB focuses on supporting OLAP on *fresh data* but not necessarily the latest version of the data.

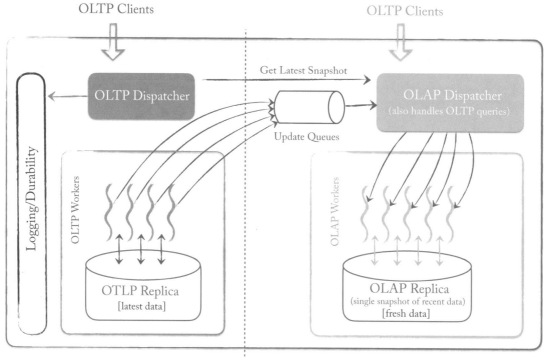

Figure 5.11: The BatchDB architecture supports hybrid OLAP and OLTP workloads.

5.2.4   DEUTERONOMY: DECOMPOSED TRANSACTION MODEL

Levandoski et al. [76] introduced a decoupled database architecture, referred to as Deuteronomy, consisting of (1) a transaction component (TC) that focuses exclusively on a logical concurrency control and oblivious about the storage layer; and (2) data component (DC) that focuses on storage and efficient access methods (e.g., indexes) having no knowledge of the transaction layer, namely, exposing a key-value interface. The overall architecture of Deuteronomy centers around the separation of concerns and is demonstrated in Figure 5.12.

The underlying concurrency model in Deuteronomy follows a multi-version timestamp ordering protocol with read range support (range writes are not supported) based on maintaining disjoint logical ranges, also a step toward combining analytical and transactional capability through querying range support. These ranges are protected using a multi-granularity hierarchi-

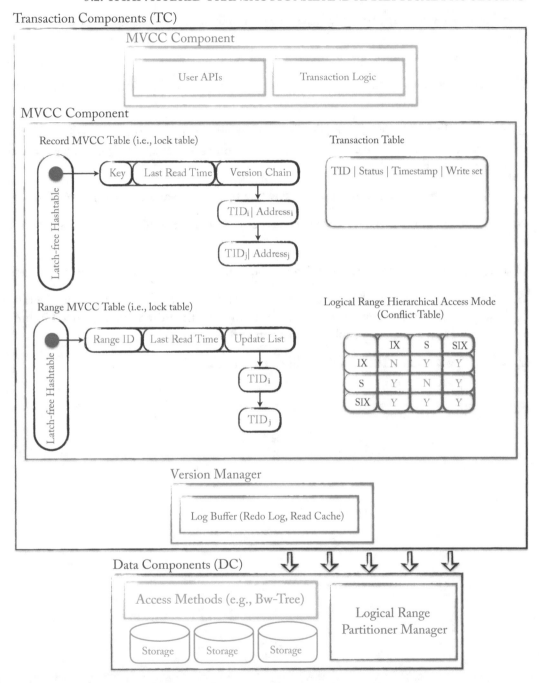

Figure 5.12: The decoupled Deuteronomy architecture has distinct transaction and data components (separation of concerns).

cal locking scheme that supports only IX, S, and SIX lock modes. The range meta-data includes the last read time and outstanding locks which are efficiently stored using a latch-free hash table, referred to as Range MVCC table in Figure 5.12. The Deuteronomy protocol is the following:

1. When transaction T_i starts, the timestamp c_i is assigned to T_i which serves as both start time and commit time.

2. Any record with timestamp smaller than c_i is visible to T_i; any time T_i reads a record, it updates the last read time of the record to c_i assuming no newer transactions have already read the record.

3. If T_i encounters an uncommitted record with a timestamp smaller than c_i, then T_i aborts.

4. If T_i attempts to write a record which has the last read time smaller than c_i, then again T_i aborts.

5. If T_i attempts to write a record with an outstanding uncommitted write, again T_i aborts.

6. When T_i attempts to update the record r, it requests an intention (IX) lock on the range holding r. If the range last read time is larger than c_i, then the write is rejected in order to avoid reader's range repeatability violation and phantoms.

7. When T_i commits, all of its writes will receive time c_i.

CHAPTER 6

Hardware-Assisted Transactional Utilities

Many crucial components of a transaction processing system are orthogonal to the design of the concurrency control kernel. Such utility modules in a transactional system automatically perform database partitioning (sharding) and index data for efficient accesses. This chapter describes different designs, which are often complementary, for data partitioning and indexing.

6.1 DATABASE PARTITIONING

Many transaction processing workloads exhibit an access pattern that is easy to predict. This, for example, is the case when a transaction is installed as a stored procedure and the records it accesses are solely determined by the parameter values that are passed to the stored procedure. In addition, the accesses can often be predicted because of known relationships between objects, such as a hierarchy between bank branches and accounts, customers and orders, or suppliers and parts. A predictable access pattern allows a transaction processing system to partition the records in the database such that most transactions will only access a single partition. Leveraging this property allows for concurrency control protocols that are much simpler, and much faster, than protocols for general workloads.

6.1.1 SCHISM

Partition-based approaches are very efficient if one can devise a good partitioning strategy. This may be challenging even for domain experts, however, as the properties of the query workload may not be in advance. Schism [27] has proposed an automated method to create a partitioning scheme for a given database and query workload. In particular, Schism introduces a database partitioner that attempts to minimize the number of distributed transactions while producing balanced partitions.

Schism models workload partitioning as a graph problem. Nodes in the graph represent tuples, and edges between nodes represent accesses of the two tuples by the same transaction. Modeling the transactional activity as a graph assumes *a priori* knowledge of the read and write sets as well as knowledge of the transaction classes and execution frequencies of each class.

A challenge is that the size of the graph may become unmanageable, as the number of nodes in the graph is proportional to the size of the database and the number of edges is proportional to the number of transactions that are being analyzed. Schism applies sampling techniques to selectively trace transactions, which reduces the number of edges of the graph. In addition, some tuples may always be accessed together, which will form a clique in the graph. One can coalesce such joint accesses and represent them with a single node.

Schism seeks to calculate n balanced partitions on the transactional activity graph by minimizing inter-partition traffic. This requires performing n min-cuts to the graph, which can be done by modeling the cost of different viable graph partitionings that are produced by a k-way graph partitioning algorithm. Schism uses the METIS framework by Karypis and Kumar for this purpose [59] (see Figure 6.1).

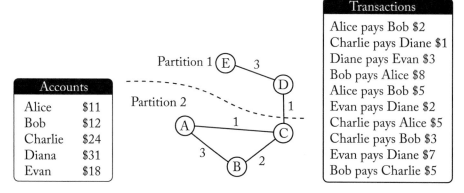

Figure 6.1: Graph representation of transactional activity in Schism. Schism forms k partitions by performing $k - 1$ minimum cuts on this graph.

6.1.2   ZEPHYR

A disadvantage of offline partitioning techniques is that they are not cognizant to unpredictable changes to the query workload that occur at runtime. For example, many OLTP workloads encounter hotspots where a small fraction of the database receives all the activity, and these hotspots change based on external factors such as the weather or the news. A static partitioning scheme can overwhelm certain CPU cores as it cannot react to runtime changes to the OLTP workload.

Zephyr migrates database partitions among nodes in a shared-nothing transactional database [34]. Zephyr uses a centralized query router that dispatches transactions to their destinations. The first step of migration is initialization, where minimal information about the schema, index structures, and authentication information is sent to the destination. Once this information has been received by the destination node, the query router will start dispatching transactions to the new destination. The migration then enters the "dual mode" phase, where the partition is assigned to both the source and destination and the two coordinate to ensure transactional correctness. New transactions are dispatched to the destination and pull pages from the source. In the meantime, transactions that were active at the source are drained. During this "dual mode" phase, active transactions at the source will abort if the page their data resides in is migrated. Finally, when all transactions at the source have completed, the source transfers ownership of the partition to the destination and pushes the remaining data.

6.1.3   SQUALL

Squall extends the idea of on-line partitioning to perform *live migration*, which means that data can be migrated without any portion of the database becoming inaccessible, however briefly [33]. Live migration requires addressing two technical challenges: (1) a transaction must always find a tuple at that partition that it currently resides in (no false negatives); and (2) a transaction must never assume a tuple exists in a partition when it does not (no false positives). Squall performs live migration in a decentralized and fault-tolerant manner, and performs a reconfiguration in three stages.

The first phase initializes data structures that will track the progress of the partition migration. Migrating tuples are represented as ranges on the partitioning attribute of a table which are stored along with the old and new partition identifiers. Each migration range can be in one of the three states: *Not started*, *Partial*, and *Complete*. Migrations cascade to all tables that have a foreign key relationship with the table. The migration ranges can be independently calculated by every node, hence tracking this information does not require synchronization or global state.

The second phase performs the migration. While a migration range is in transit to its new destination (that is, the range is in the *Partial* state), a transaction will be dispatched to the destination and consult the data structures that store the current location of the tuples. Any tuples that have not yet arrived to the destination will be retrieved before this transaction starts. This on-demand pull retrieves active tuples first and requires no external synchronization.

The third and final phase identifies when the migration has terminated. The source and the destination nodes determine individually if they have sent or received all the data that is needed. A successful migration is communicated to the leader who notifies nodes to remove any migration-tracking data structures.

6.1.4   E-STORE

The partitioning strategy of an OLTP workload may also need to be changed for performance reasons, as the load on the database system changes with time. This necessitates finer-grained partitioning to many CPU cores in periods of high load and coarse-grained partitioning to few CPU cores in periods of light transactional activity.

E-Store is a partitioning framework for distributed OLTP workloads that can automatically repartition in response to demand spikes or gradual changes to the OLTP load. E-Store collects system-level metrics regarding the CPU utilization of a partition to decide whether to perform a migration. If the CPU utilization is outside a range defined by a high and low watermark, E-Store identifies an imbalance that it attempts to correct. Once an imbalance is detected, E-Store switches to tuple-level monitoring to determine if there are hot spots that disproportionally contribute to the elevated load. A migration is modeled as an integer programming problem that places every tuple in a single partition and constraints the partition load to be within a narrow user-defined load target band. Solving this "bin packing" problem as an integer optimization problem is prohibitively expensive in practice; hence, E-Store turns to approximate algorithms to determine good migration strategies quickly.

6.1.5   CLAY

Clay [120] determines how to form partitions and at what nodes to transfer them for adaptive, on-line partitioning. For this purpose, Clay constructs a heat graph at runtime where node and edge weights represent the access and co-access frequency, respectively. Clay monitors the transactional activity of the system to update this graph at runtime. The partitioning strategy that Clay produces can then be executed by a live reconfiguration system like Squall [33].

Clay starts from a known partitioning scheme, which may have been produced statically, and then modifies partitions by carefully considering which tuples to migrate across partitions. Clay chooses which tuples to migrate by solving an incremental data placement problem that seeks to minimize the amount of data movement across partitions such that the load imbalance between partitions is limited. Clay defines the partition load as a sum of the weights of each node and every outgoing edge of the partition.

Clay performs a migration by forming "clumps," or groups of tuples that should be migrated as one batch. A clump is formed using a heuristic that considers migrating the node with the highest weight (the "hottest" node) in an overloaded partition. The clump is then expanded to include tuples that are co-accessed together with the node that is considered for migration. The search procedure can expand to additional nodes as needed. Once the clump has been formed that will reduce the load of this partition, Clay determines what the ideal destination would be such that the load is more balanced. By changing the number of target partitions to be greater than or less than the current number of partitions, Clay can both "scale out" and "scale in" a cluster to use more or fewer nodes, respectively.

6.2   DATABASE INDEXING

Database systems that are optimized for in-memory transactions do not organize data in a traditional buffer pool, as this carries a number of disadvantages. First, a buffer pool tracks pages and updating pages requires costly coordination, often through locks [50]. Lock-based synchronization is blocking, so threads need to context switch until the lock is granted. The overhead of context switching (or spinning) can be microseconds, which is comparable to the time it takes to complete the entire in-memory transaction. Therefore, conflicts on buffer pool locks significantly underutilize a modern CPU during in-memory transaction processing. In addition, the buffer pool can be a source of spurious lock conflicts: non-conflicting requests that access different tuples in the same page would be needlessly blocked.

Storage methods that are optimized for in-memory transactions avoid locking when reading data. Research has focused on two families of data structures, namely hash-based data structures that use a hash function to determine the access location, and tree-based data structures that organize data hierarchically. In general, hash-based data structures have the advantage of faster lookups when accessing a single key as they can directly access the data, while tree-based structures outperform with sequential accesses as they benefit from spatial and temporal locality.

6.2.1 HASH TABLES

One family of storage methods for in-memory transaction processing is hash-based indexing using hash tables. Multiple variants of hash-based structures have been proposed. This section describes the hash-based index as it has been proposed for data storage for the Hekaton main-memory transaction processing system [28].

An in-memory hash table is first created by hashing an indexable attribute of every tuple in a table. Figure 6.2 shows one such example. Every hash bucket is the root of a singly linked list that stores all the tuples that hash to the same value. For example, in Figure 6.2, the indexable attribute is "name" and we assume that the hash function h only considers the first letter of the name. Records "Alice" and "Charlie" are hashed under different buckets, $h(\text{"A"})$ and $h(\text{"C"})$, respectively, hence both records are stored in separate singly-linked chains. There is a hash collision for records "Bob" and "Beth" as both records will be stored in the same hash bucket $h(\text{"B"})$. One can find both records in the same chain in the hash table in any order.

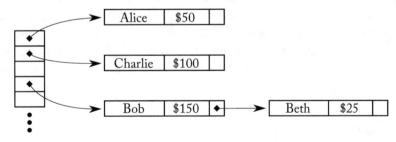

Figure 6.2: A database with four tuples stored in a hash-based index on attribute "name."

Hash-based indexes avoid spurious conflicts during concurrent operations by tracking tuples individually: as long as every operation accesses elements on different chains, all operations can proceed in parallel. The quality of the hash function is very important, however, because minimizing hash collisions maximizes concurrency. When two operations access the same chain, the singly linked list allows for lock-free modifications on the hash table. Reads start their search at the hash table bucket and follow pointers to the next data item until they reach the end of the chain. Updates can modify the pointers in the linked list using atomic compare-and-swap

(CAS) instructions. Note that the lock-free nature of this data structure guarantees *atomicity*, which means that a newly inserted record will be either seen or not seen by a reader that follows the list of pointers in a chain. There is no guarantee about the *order* in which insertions and deletions become visible to readers. In particular, an insert operation may complete successfully but may not be visible by a read that completes shortly after.

This hash-based data structure also requires lock-free memory allocation to completely avoid blocking and lock contention. A lock-free memory allocator guarantees progress regardless of the scheduling policy of different threads. Some threads, in fact, may be substantially delayed or even terminated by the operating system. Prior work has investigated how memory allocators can be designed to offer freedom from deadlocks, gracefully handle asynchronous signals and priority inversion, and tolerate thread preemption and thread termination [87].

Another related challenge is performing safe and lock-free memory reclamation when an object is deleted. In particular, the problem is how to free memory in a lock-free manner and guarantee that no thread currently accesses this memory through a pointer. One solution from prior work keeps the pointers that a thread accesses in a globally visible structure and carefully monitors when a reclamation is safe [86].

One can also build an index on multiple attributes of a table. Each indexable attribute will create a separate set of root pointers in the in-memory hash table. An example is shown in Figure 6.3 where there are two indexes: one on the "name" attribute and one on the "balance" attribute. Note that the tuples now store two pointers: the first is the pointer that traverses chains that are indexed on "name" and the second is the pointer that traverses chains that are indexed on "balance." An implication of having multiple indexes on the same table is that an insertion can never be performed atomically on all indexes, as the pointers need to be set in some order. Hence, a reader that accesses data from one index may not encounter some tuple when accessing the other index. For example, assume that the tuple (Charlie, \$100) is being inserted. A reader following the $h($"C"$)$ chain may encounter the tuple, while a reader following the $h(\$100)$ chain may not. The transaction processing kernel needs to compensate for this deficiency to ensure serializability.

6.2.2 BW-TREE

The Bw-tree is a tree-based in-memory data structure [77]. A Bw-tree organizes data in pages. Pages in the Bw-tree contain key and pointer pairs to direct searches to lower levels of the Bw-tree. The keys in every page are sorted. Leaf pages in a Bw-tree contain a key and value pairs. All pages contain a side (link) pointer that points to the immediate right sibling on the same level of the tree to support fast scans. The Bw-tree closely resembles the B^{link}-tree data structure [74] which is characterized by its "sideways" pointer that connects pages at the same level of the tree.

The Bw-tree offers logarithmic access time for key lookups. After the first lookup, range queries on the indexed key range can be answered in linear time. Compared to a hash table, accessing one key is more expensive as it requires multiple lookups in the mapping table. However,

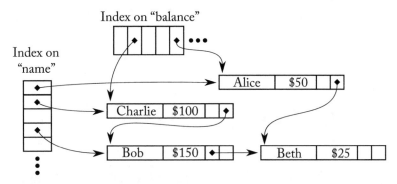

Figure 6.3: A database with four tuples and two hash-based indexes: one on attribute "name" and another on attribute "balance." The example assumes $h(\$100)= h(\$150)$ and $h(\$50)= h(\$25)$.

range queries in Bw-tree are more efficient than performing multiple accesses to a hash table as they access contiguous data items.

A Bw-tree is shown in Figure 6.4. The main distinction from disk-oriented tree structures is that all page references in the Bw-tree are *logical references* to a page identifier LPID. This indirection table, called a mapping table, is a hash table that is shown on the left in Figure 6.4. The mapping table maintains the current mapping of logical page identifiers to physical memory locations. Consider a lookup for the first record under key "B". The first access is at the root of the Bw-tree that accesses page R with a logical identifier of 0x20C. The root page contains three keys ("A", "B", and "C") and their respective pointers in the form of logical page identifiers. The next level of pages can be accessed by looking up the memory address corresponding to the logical page identifier in the mapping table. In our example, the page of interest for the record under key "B" is the page with a logical identifier of 0x430.

Updates in a Bw-tree never modify the contents of a page. Instead, updates create delta records that are prepended to existing pages and describe the update. For example, in Figure 6.4, an insertion into page A produces the delta page Δ. Readers accessing page A will do so through its logical page identifier 0x1AF. Hence, readers will encounter page Δ first and apply the update (in this case, an insert) when reading page A. The memory address of the delta page is atomically installed in the mapping table using the compare-and-swap (CAS) instruction.

The ability to access pages through an indirection table allows readers to access the Bw-tree in a lock-free manner. A concurrent read request that looks up the physical location of a logical page identifier in the mapping table will never see an inconsistent state: a read request will either see the new page address (that contains the delta record) or the old page address (that skips the delta record). Periodically, the system consolidates Bw-tree pages with multiple delta records into a single page for efficiency. Pages in a Bw-tree have no fixed size and they can become arbitrarily large until they are split.

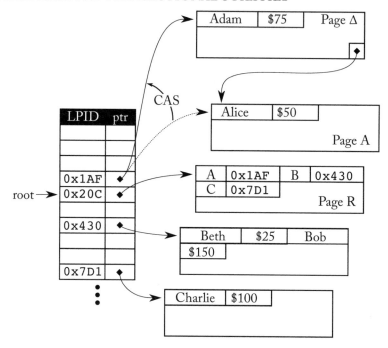

Figure 6.4: The Bw-tree resembles a B-tree that uses a *logical page identifier* to refer to every page instead of a pointer. New updates do not update in place, but instead produce a *delta* page Δ that is prepended to the chain using an atomic compare-and-swap (CAS) instruction.

The Bw-tree has been extended to use hardware transactional memory and multi-word CAS operations by Makreshanski et al. [83]. A challenge with multi-word operations is the possibility of repeated failures of a multi-word CAS operation in the presence of high contention. The two options are infinitely retrying or reverting to a global lock mechanism to impose some ordering between conflicting operations. Both solutions incur a performance penalty over lock-free approaches that use single-word CAS. Using hardware transactional memory, however, greatly reduces the coding complexity.

6.2.3   MASSTREE

A tree-based in-memory data structure is Masstree [85]. Masstree combines properties of a trie and a B+-tree in one data structure. The Silo transaction processing engine uses Masstree for data storage [132].

A Masstree consists of multiple trees arranged in layers. Each layer is indexed by an 8-byte slice of the key. Layer 0 in Figure 6.5 is a single tree that is indexed by bytes 0–7 of the key; trees in layer 1, the next deeper layer, are indexed by bytes 8–15; trees in layer 2 by bytes 16–23; and so forth. Each tree contains interior nodes and border (leaf) nodes. Interior nodes (shown in white in Figure 6.5) form the trie, whereas border nodes (shown in gray in Figure 6.5) are akin to the nodes of a B+-tree that store data or pointers to trees in deeper layers. Masstree creates additional layers as needed when an insertion cannot use an existing tree.

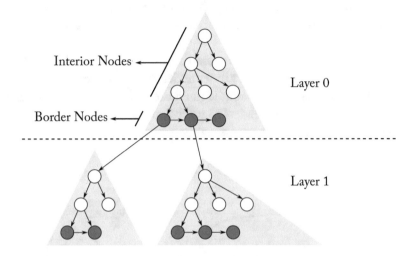

Figure 6.5: Masstree combines properties of a trie and a B+-tree in one data structure.

Masstree coordinates writes for high concurrency. Instead of a lock, each node in the Masstree structure has a version counter. A writer increments the version counter of a node to denote an in-progress update, and increments the version number again after the update has been installed. Readers coordinate with writers by checking the version of a node before a read and comparing this number to the version after the operation. If the two version numbers differ or a version number is an odd number, the reader may have observed an inconsistent state and will retry. Therefore, conflicting requests in Masstree may restart but readers will never write globally-accessible shared memory.

6.2.4   ART: THE ADAPTIVE RADIX TREE

ART is an adaptive radix tree (trie) for indexing data in main memory [75]. Each layer of an ART index stores one-byte slice of the key. Inner nodes map partial keys to child pointers, while leaf nodes store the key and the associated value.

Inner nodes in ART have a fanout of either 4, 16, 48, or 256. ART uses different data structures for inner nodes based on their fanout. Nodes with fanout of 4 store four keys and four child pointers in separate arrays. A reader that encounters a 4-entry node performs a key comparison with each of the four keys, and only follows a child pointer if the comparison with its key was successful. The same node layout is used for nodes with a fanout of 16, albeit the internal structures are sized to store 16 child pointers and their respective keys. By storing the keys separately from the pointers, the key comparison can be accelerated using vector instructions such as `PCMPEQB`. Nodes with a fanout of 48 stores 48 child pointers and one 256-element index array. At most, 48 entries in this index array are not `NULL`. The lookup key is used as an offset to access the 256-element array, and the value in this array returns the appropriate child pointer that needs to be followed for this lookup key. Nodes with a fanout of 256 nodes do not use an index array: the lookup key will be used as an offset to directly access the appropriate child pointer.

In addition, ART employs path compression optimizations to avoid creating long chains of internal nodes. In particular, ART creates inner nodes only if they are necessary to distinguish between two or more leaf nodes. In the example in Figure 6.6, the key "air" does not require the intermediate node for "r". This allows readers to reach leaf nodes as soon as the unique prefix of each key has been traversed, instead of traversing the entire chain.

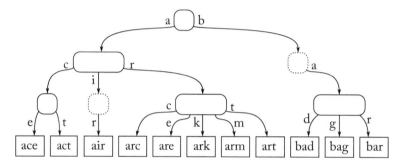

Figure 6.6: ART is a radix tree that adapts the size of internal nodes based on their fanout.

ART can also compress paths between internal nodes as long as the path does not contain a branch. In Figure 6.6, the "ba" search prefix is such a compressible path. ART compresses such paths by removing intermediate nodes and storing the length of the removed path at the node at the end of the path. The length indicates to readers how many bytes of the lookup key they need to discard before performing a key comparison. A challenge with this approach is that the compressed path may introduce spurious key matches. For example, in Figure 6.6, a lookup for the key "bed" will arrive at the leaf node "bad." To avoid this problem, readers that encountered a compressed path during their traversal in ART must verify that the final key matches the searched key at the end of every lookup.

The performance of the ART index has been thoroughly evaluated by Alvarez et al. for both OLAP and OLTP scenarios [3]. Experimental results show that ART is an efficient radix tree, but its performance can be slower than efficient in-memory hashing techniques based on quadratic probing and cuckoo hashing.

6.2.5   BZTREE

The BzTree is a B+-tree that is designed for efficiency and persistence using non-volatile memory [6]. Like a B+-tree, internal BzTree nodes store search keys and pointers to child nodes and leaf BzTree nodes store keys and payload values or pointers. The BzTree uses latch-free operations for performance and uses non-volatile memory for near-instantaneous recovery.

The BzTree relies on PMwCAS, a persistent multi-word compare-and-swap (CAS) primitive that is implemented in software. PMwCAS has been introduced by Wang et al. [135] and uses a shared descriptor table that is accessible by all threads. The descriptor table records sequences of operations that are carried out using a single-word CAS and are persisted using cache line flush (CLFLUSH) and write back (CLWB) instructions.

A BzTree node uses a slotted page layout, as shown in Figure 6.7. A header and fixed-size record metadata M_i are stored at the beginning of the page, while variable-length records KV_i are added "backward" from the end of the page toward the beginning. A record KV_i stores a variable-length key and a variable-length value. (The value is a payload for leaf nodes or a child pointer for internal nodes.) A metadata entry M_i is 8 bytes long and stores control data ctrl for PMwCAS, a visibility flag v that controls the visibility of the record, an offset to the record KV_i, and the length of the key and the record in bytes. The header of a BzTree node is 16 bytes and stores: (1) the size of the entire node; (2) control data ctrl for use by PMwCAS; (3) a frozen flag fz to mark the node as immutable; (4) the blksz field that keeps the length of the record block (all KV_i records of this node); (5) the delsz field that keeps the amount of logically deleted space on the node; and (6) a sorted count value that is used as an index to records that were recently added to the node and whose keys are currently unsorted.

New records are inserted in the free space in the node using a 2-word PMwCAS. The first CAS is on the header to update the count and blksz fields. The second CAS creates a new record metadata entry M_i. If the PMwCAS operation is successful, the writer marks the record as invisible in M_i and proceeds to populate the record entry KV_i and flush it for persistence. The record is made visible by another two-word PMwCAS operation that sets the visibility flag in M_i and overwrites the fz, count, and blksz fields with their current value. This is done to detect a race with concurrent operations that set the immutability flag fz to modify the tree structure. If fz has been modified, the inserter must restart the operation and re-traverse the BzTree from the root so as to reach a new, mutable page that can be used for record insertion.

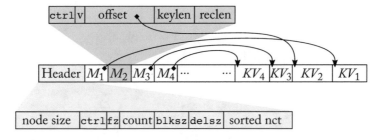

Figure 6.7: A node of the BzTree, a B+-tree with fast persistence and recovery using non-volatile memory.

Periodically, the system performs node consolidation that reclaims deleted space and inserts all newly added (and unsorted) keys in the sorted record block.

Reads in BzTree are performed using the standard B+-tree search logic. Within a node, a reader performs a binary search for the desired key on the sorted record space, and if no match is not found the reader then sequentially compares keys in the unsorted record space. Readers ignore concurrent update activity by disregarding the immutability flag `fz` and any invisible records. Hence, the BzTree design ensures that updates don't block readers. However, the BzTree does not guarantee the transactional serializability of concurrent operations, which must be handled independently by the caller.

CHAPTER 7

Transactions on Heterogeneous Hardware

The hardware trends described in Chapter 1 suggest that future hardware will be increasingly more heterogeneous and reconfigurable to accommodate for domain-specific or problem-specific processing needs. To ensure uniformity in communication between discrete hardware units with different roles, data transmissions will largely be through memory-centric interfaces with the capability to directly access memory either locally (DMA) or remotely (RDMA). A natural question to ask is how will transaction processing systems leverage heterogeneity and efficiently access data in a network of heterogeneous systems. This chapter describes some research results in this direction.

7.1   HARDWARE ACCELERATORS

Some very promising research has considered field-programmable gate arrays (FPGAs) and graphic processing units (GPUs) as hardware accelerators for transaction processing systems.

Unlike regular circuits that are pre-fabricated before deployment, FPGAs can be configured (and reconfigured) after deployment. This allows a designer to customize the FPGA for a particular problem or workload through a hardware description language. Because of their reconfigurability, FPGAs bridge the gap between the flexibility of software and the performance of traditional integrated circuits. Although an FPGA is neither as flexible as software nor as fast as an integrated circuit, recent research suggests that FPGAs have a unique role to play in a modern datacenter.

Graphic processing units were originally designed to accelerate the manipulation of the frame buffer that will be displayed on the screen. Their architecture was designed to meet hard real-time constraints for humans to perceive a series of discrete images as uninterruptible motion. In addition, modern GPUs use specialized circuits to perform calculations that are common in 3D graphics and video processing, such as large matrix and vector operations. This unique architecture makes GPUs well suited for embarrassingly parallel problems. A growing body of research is examining how to leverage GPUs for other domains, including transaction processing.

7.1.1   FPGA ACCELERATION FOR DISTRIBUTED CONSENSUS

Data consistency in distributed systems often relies on distributed consensus. Yet, consensus is an expensive operation, as it requires multiple rounds of communication to reach an agreement: a decision can be taken only as quickly as the network round-trip time. Agreement protocols can thus quickly become bottlenecks.

Istvàn et al. show that consensus can be accelerated by offloading it to specialized hardware [53]. Specifically, they implement Zookeeper's atomic broadcast in an FPGA that can run a TCP/IP network stack. The consensus module separates the control and the data planes, which are routed to the Control State Machine and the Log/Data Manager. Both components work in parallel to reduce latency. The consensus module is pipelined, so it is possible to have multiple outstanding requests in flight.

The benefit of accelerating consensus using an FPGA in the network is that one can leverage the predictable performance of datacenter networks, where message latencies are bound and predictable. This allows parameters like timeouts for leader election to be much lower than what would be feasible in software alone. Hence, in practice distributed consensus in an FPGA performs much closer to the ideal performance than the worst-case performance.

7.1.2   FPGA ACCELERATION FOR DATA STREAMING

The Flexible Query Processor (FQP) is a collection of stream-based hardware processing blocks that can be inter-connected into a topology to process data streams [89–93, 114]. FQP is prototyped on FPGAs, but unlike prior FPGA-based approaches, it does not require re-synthesizing the blocks when the query or the schema of the data change. In addition, changes to the query or the data stream are supported during active processing without requiring an expensive reconfiguration of the FPGA.

A data stream in FQP is processed using a workload-specific topology of processing blocks, as shown in Figure 7.1. In addition to processing blocks, the topology contains blocks for query and tuple buffering, routing, and dispatching. An incoming tuple is propagated to the next pipeline stage on each clock cycle until it reaches the end of the path. A tuple can be propagated to multiple blocks after each pipeline stage. Adding more blocks after a pipeline stage can lengthen the clock cycle and hence decrease the clock frequency of the FPGA, which will degrade performance. FQP imposes a device-specific maximum fan-out to mitigate this problem.

FQP is designed to minimize pipeline stalls. Stalls during processing are introduced when a block wants to propagate tuples to a block that is busy processing previous tuples. A special Buffer/DMUX block buffers incoming tuples and forwards them to the next block. Another source of pipeline stalls is pushing results to the output port. FQP implements a Result Aggregation Buffer (RAB) with a fairness policy that seeks to avoid starvation.

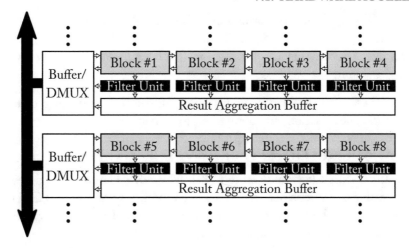

Figure 7.1: FQP processes data by constructing a topology of pre-defined processing blocks. When the query or the schema changes, FQP does not require re-synthesizing the blocks.

7.1.3 Q100, A DATABASE PROCESSING UNIT

Q100 is a domain-specific processor to efficiently handle database queries [141, 142]. Q100 implements common operators, such as join or sort, as fixed-function ASIC tiles. The instruction set architecture of Q100 captures the producer/consumer relationships between relational operations in a query plan. Q100 is a VLIW architecture and the basic instruction in Q100 implements standard SQL operations, such as select, join, aggregate, partition and sort. When a query does not fit on the available Q100 tiles, it must be split into multiple instructions which will be executed sequentially. The Q100 microarchitecture revolves around the following 11 operations which directly map to dedicated hardware tiles on the Q100 chip:

Sorter tile: The tile sorts the input using bitonic sort.

Partitioner tile: The partitioner splits large tables into smaller tables. Q100 implements range partitioning due to its tolerance of irregular data distributions.

Joiner tile: The tile performs an equijoin between two tables on a primary key and a foreign key.

Arithmetic and logic tile: This tile evaluates arithmetic and logical operations on two input columns and produces one column at the output.

Boolean generator tile: This tile compares a column with a constant or another column.

Column filter tile: The column filter takes two inputs: (1) a data column and (2) a Boolean column. This tile outputs the data column and drops rows for which the value in the Boolean column is false.

Aggregator tile: The aggregator performs a SQL "group by" on an input column. Aggregating requires saving the partial aggregates for each group, which requires allocating a buffer of unknown size. To solve this, this tile requires that both input columns arrive sorted on the "group by" column.

Auxiliary tiles: These tiles perform auxiliary operations such as selecting columns, column stitching and concatenation, and appending to a table.

7.1.4 GPU ACCELERATION FOR KEY-VALUE STORES

Mega-KV is a GPU-based key-value store [148]. Mega-KV claims throughput that exceeds 160 million key-value operations per second on a commodity system with 2 GPUs. The design of Mega-KV is based on the following unique characteristics of key-value workloads: (1) they require high memory bandwidth to process many concurrent requests; (2) they can accommodate massive data parallelism with simple compute; and (3) they poorly utilize the CPU cache as the working set is large. Mega-KV leverages the high bandwidth of GPUs, but it needs to carefully hide the higher latency of accessing the GPU over the PCI-X bus while offering bounded response latency.

Mega-KV uses GPUs as a special-purpose accelerator for key-value stores. Using GPUs requires strictly limiting the memory footprint in what can fit in the limited GPU memory, as accessing host memory would require expensive round-trips in the PCI-X bus. Mega-KV decouples indexing from key-value storage: the index is kept in the small but fast GPU memory while keys and values are stored in the larger but slower host memory. Mega-KV uses a GPU-optimized version of cuckoo hashing with two hash functions and a large number of cells per hash bucket. Cuckoo hashing was chosen due to its high load factor (i.e., high memory utilization) and constant lookup time.

The workflow of Mega-KV is shown in Figure 7.2. Mega-KV schedules operations in batches, which are applied separately for each type of operation (Search, Insert, and Delete). As Search operations dominate many key-value store workloads, Insert and Delete batches are scheduled less frequently than Search batches. To limit response latency, Mega-KV schedules operations in a fixed cycle and not necessarily when a batch is full. Each operation arrives through a high-speed network and is placed in a buffer. Receiver threads work on the CPU to batch incoming queries. A CUDA stream is launched to process the buffer of each Receiver for GPU execution. After the GPU kernel terminates, the buffer is assigned to a Sender thread for post-processing in the CPU. When post-processing completes, the Sender clears each buffer for reuse. By swapping buffers, the overhead of copying between pipeline stages is eliminated, except for CPU-GPU transfers.

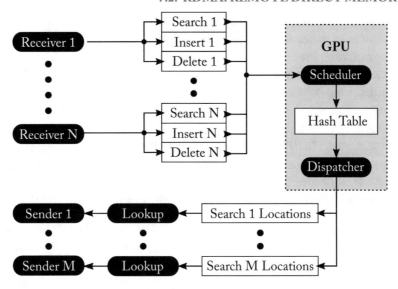

Figure 7.2: The workflow of Mega-KV, a GPU-accelerated key-value store.

7.2   RDMA: REMOTE DIRECT MEMORY ACCESS

High-performance network protocols such as InfiniBand, RoCE, and iWARP offer low-latency and high-bandwidth communication, and provide remote memory access (RDMA) capabilities that allow applications to directly access memory in remote computers. Modern network adapters expose memory semantics to applications using RDMA and offer very high throughput. 200 Gbps InfiniBand devices are available today and 400 Gbps is the next industry milestone. Ethernet is quickly closing the gap with 100 Gbps speeds and RDMA support. While the bandwidth has quadrupled across generations of network adaptors, latency has stubbornly remained a little over 1 μs per round-trip. The laws of physics suggest that latency is unlikely to improve further.

What is remarkable is the pace at which fast networks are gaining broader market acceptance. For an investment of about $1,000 per port, commodity servers today can communicate at speeds that were only achievable in high-end supercomputers only a few years ago. The biggest benefit to applications from the commoditization of fast networking is standardization, which promises performance portability across deployments.

RDMA allows applications to use message-passing mechanisms or shared memory abstractions to access remote memory. Message-oriented communication is cooperative: the receiver initiates the communication and specifies a location in its memory space that will be changed; then the sender determines what to change in the receiver's memory space and completes the data transfer. A shared-memory abstraction allows one of the two sides to remain completely passive. For this reason, one-sided communication primitives such as RDMA Read and RDMA Write have generated substantial research excitement.

What programming interfaces do applications use to access an RDMA-capable network? The TCP/IP stack copies data from kernel memory to user memory during a data transfer and is typically avoided. One solution is MPI, a de facto standard in the high-performance computing community. However, MPI is far from a perfect solution for data-intensive processing. In addition, debugging performance problems is cumbersome, as the MPI library is opaque to applications. Furthermore, MPI imposes limitations to the memory management decisions that are made by the application. Many data-intensive applications increasingly opt to use the Open-Fabrics Verbs interface (libibverbs) and directly access the network adapter. The Verbs interface supports two communication modes for applications: the channel mode and the memory mode.

Channel mode: In this mode, applications eschew the ability to directly access remote memory and instead send or receive messages. This turns out to be a very efficient way to communicate, especially when used with an unreliable datagram protocol. Using a fast network as a message channel is not a panacea, however, because the receiver has to initiate the message transmission. (Otherwise, the network adapter would not know the user space address where it can store an incoming message.) Communicating in the channel mode requires coordination in software to ensure that receivers are ready to receive messages before senders transmit them. This may require substantial algorithmic changes or even be infeasible for certain applications. Furthermore, applications using an unreliable datagram protocol now need to tolerate out of order message delivery, carefully tune the window size, avoid "buffer bloat" and network congestion, and gracefully recover when packets are dropped—all are features of the TCP/IP stack that applications have come to take for granted.

Memory mode: The alternative is to use the memory mode to transfer data, where applications will directly read from and write to remote memory. The technical challenge is that the latency of a remote memory access is one order of magnitude greater than the latency of a local memory access. Remote manipulations of even the simplest data structures require multiple round-trips in the network, in either a "lock, write, unlock" or a lock-free "fetch-and-add, then write" pattern. The overall latency of such an operation would likely be in the 10 μs range. The application needs to be implemented cleverly to hide such microsecond-long latencies, which itself is a challenging, open problem.

7.2.1   RAMCLOUD

RAMCloud is a distributed data store that keeps all data in DRAM at all times [97]. Applications that connect to RAMCloud access data as if it is stored in a single, coherent and consistent key-value store. RAMCloud enforces durability by keeping backup copies in log-structured storage. Read operations in RAMCloud take under 5 μs and write operations under 15 μs. The majority of the time in a read operation goes to the delay in transmitting packets in a fast network, as accessing data in a round-trip communication takes at least 2 μs in small clusters with negligible switching overheads. This leaves only a few microseconds for processing. RAMCloud is carefully designed to avoid the following sources of processing latency and performance variability.

1. **No kernel calls during communication:** RAMCloud directly communicates with the NIC and bypasses the kernel to send and receive messages. This is achieved by using the InfiniBand verbs API, which allows applications to directly access RDMA-capable NICs. RAMCloud uses message passing and receivers continuously poll for new messages.

2. **No lock-based synchronization:** Acquiring and releasing a cached, non-contended lock takes about 20 ns. If the lock needs to be retrieved from memory, a single lock access will take ten times longer and contention will introduce unbounded wait times. RAMCloud is designed with the goal of minimizing inter-thread synchronization.

3. **Strict CPU cache miss budget:** The strict micro-second processing budget requires performing less than ten cache misses in the common case. Data-dependent accesses are particularly problematic and are avoided in RAMCloud.

4. **No batching:** Batching amortizes the overhead of operations but adds unpredictable latency to requests if one waits for a batch to be filled. As RAMCloud optimizes for latency and not throughput, batching is not performed.

Data in RAMCloud is divided into tables, and each table consists of objects. An object in RAMCloud is a (key, value, version) tuple. Objects have a unique, variable-length key (up to 64 KB), a variable-length value (up to 1 MB) and an 8-byte version number that is uniquely assigned by RAMCloud to every write for this key. RAMCloud supports metadata operations (table creation, table deletion), object operations (read, write and delete) and bulk operations (multi-read, multi-write, multi-delete and iteration over all objects in the table). In addition, RAMCloud supports two atomic operations, conditional write and increment. There is no support for transactions in RAMCloud v1.0, so the atomicity of a sequence of operations needs to be protected by the application using the two atomic primitives provided by RAMCloud.

7.2.2   FARM: FAST REMOTE MEMORY

FaRM: Fast Remote Memory is a distributed computing platform that uses main memory for data storage [31]. FaRM exposes remote memory as a shared, global memory space. Applications can allocate, read, write, and free objects in this space while being oblivious to the physical location of the object (Figure 7.3).

Communication in FaRM is one-directional and uses the RDMA Read and RDMA Write transport functions. A sender communicates with the receiver through a circular buffer that is stored in the receiver. The sender populates the circular buffer by issuing RDMA Write requests, while the receiver polls the "head" position of the buffer for new messages. The "head"

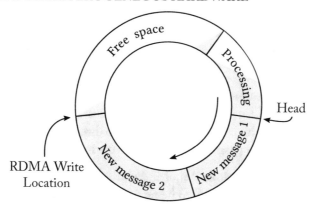

Figure 7.3: A circular buffer in FaRM. New messages are written using RDMA Write to the end of the buffer, while the local process consumes messages from the "head" pointer.

pointer is incremented when the message is assigned for processing. Once the receiver processes the message, it is cleared to make room for future messages.

Transactional Support

FaRM provides a serializable transactional interface for applications. Operations to the global shared memory are grouped into transactions. A Read operation reads an object given its address and its size. A Read uses RDMA to read data into a local buffer. To update an object, a transaction must first read the object and then perform a Write operation. The Write operation creates a copy of the local buffer and modifies the object data. The readset and the writeset of a transaction is updated on every Read and Write operation to reflect all the operations of a transaction so far.

Applications make writes visible and persistent by committing the transaction. At commit, the machine that started the transaction acts as the coordinator. The coordinator sends "prepare" messages to all nodes in the write set to lock the modified objects. After it receives an acknowledgment from all participants, the coordinator sends "validate" messages to all nodes in the read set to verify if the versions read are up to date. If validation succeeds, the coordinator sends "commit" messages to all participants. Transactions in FaRM can abort due to validation failures or for failure to receive a reply to a message.

Consistent, Lock-free Reads

Distributed transactions are often too expensive for applications. FaRM implements consistent lock-free reads that are serializable with transactions. A lock-free operation is bracketed by calls to *start* and *end* functions that denote the boundaries of the critical segment. The *start* function reads the object header, checks if the object is unlocked, and reads the version number. The *end* function verifies that the version number has not changed, guaranteeing the consistency of the entire read within this transaction.

Object Allocation, Co-location, and Addressing
The application first needs to create a transaction context to allocate and free objects. Object allocation returns a 64-bit pointer that can be persisted in data structures. Internally, FaRM splits this 64-bit pointer into a 32-bit *region identifier* and a 32-bit memory offset relative to the start of the region. To access an object, FaRM implements consistent hashing using a one-hop distributed hashtable to map the region identifier to a machine address.

Applications can request new objects to be co-located at the same machine as an existing object by passing the pointer of the existing object to the new object allocation function. This allows carefully constructed applications to co-locate data and perform single-site transactions for partitionable transactional workloads.

7.2.3   MICA: MEMORY-STORE WITH INTELLIGENT CONCURRENT ACCESS

Memory-store with Intelligent Concurrent Access (MICA) is an in-memory key-value store that carefully optimizes the network and the local memory access path for high throughput [78]. MICA claims more than 70 million key-value operations per second from a single server. MICA achieves this performance with the following optimizations.

Data partitioning and assignment to CPU cores: MICA partitions the workload per CPU core and uses NUMA-aware memory allocation, so that each CPU only manipulates data in its local NUMA domain. MICA operates in two modes. The first mode is Exclusive Reads Exclusive Writes (EREW), where a single CPU core is assigned to each partition for all operations. The second mode is Concurrent Reads Exclusive Writes (CREW) where any CPU core can read partitions, but only a single CPU core can write to a partition.

Direct NIC access with core-level message dispatch: MICA uses Intel DPDK instead of standard socket I/O to directly control the NIC and transfer data with less overhead. MICA allocates dedicated receive and transmit queues to each CPU core. This exclusive access means that CPU cores can manipulate their local receive and transmit queues without synchronization. Instead of dispatching locally when a packet is received, the client directs requests to a particular queue from the remote side.

Amortizing transmission costs and avoiding redundant copying: MICA amortizes the cost of accessing a queue over multiple requests by performing network I/O in *bursts* of up to 32 packets. This burst I/O optimization is applied both when requesting packets from the receive queue and when transmitting packets to the send queue. Performing I/O in bursts lowers CPU utilization and allows MICA to scale better under skewed accesses (that is, when some partitions have higher traffic than others). In addition, MICA reuses packet buffers to avoid redundant copying. Every packet buffer in MICA is sized to the MTU. When a request is received, MICA uses the incoming packet buffer to construct the response and passes it as the outgoing packet buffer to the send queue.

7.2.4   PILAF

Pilaf is a distributed in-memory key-value store that leverages RDMA for low CPU overhead and high performance [88]. Pilaf clients read directly from remote memory using RMDA Read when processing a Get request. Put requests are handled at the server to simplify concurrent memory accesses. This means that local memory writes performed by the server on a Put may cause read-write conflicts with concurrent Get operations that are performed using one-sided RDMA Read operations. Specifically, an RDMA Read may access the server at a time where the data structures are in an inconsistent state.

Pilaf uses checksums to detect when an RDMA Read retrieves memory that is currently being modified by a concurrent Put request. If a race is detected, the Pilaf client will retry the operation. By using a checksum a client can detect the inconsistency between a pointer's intended memory reference and the actual memory content. Sometimes, however, the data structure needs to change fundamentally such that references to prior objects would be invalid. Examples of such operations include a hash table resizing operation. Pilaf will temporarily suspend RDMA operations during these operations by resetting all connections.

Table 7.1: The key difference between HERD, Pilaf, and Nessie is whether the server is involved in handling GET and PUT requests

	HERD	Pilaf	Nessie
Are GET requests handled as one-sided operations?	No	Yes	Yes
Are PUT requests handled as one-sided operations?	No	No	Yes

7.2.5   HERD

HERD is a key-value system that is designed for RDMA-based networks and optimizes its design to reduce the number of message round-trips in the network [56]. The design of HERD is inspired by the observation that RDMA Read operations, as used in Pilaf, often require multiple round-trips in the network. This reflects the fundamental difficulty of ensuring that a remote data structure is always consistent for remote reads. In addition, RDMA Read operations use the reliable connection (RC) transport service which requires maintaining one connection for every possible sender/receiver combination. Thus, HERD observes that RDMA Write requests achieve lower latency and higher throughput than RDMA Read requests.

HERD uses a mix of "one-sided" RDMA Write requests and "two-sided" RDMA Send/Receive requests in its design. Clients in HERD transmit requests to server memory using RDMA Write. The server polls memory for incoming requests and performs the requested Get or Put operation on the key-value store. The designers of HERD argue that having many inbound RDMA Writes scales well, as the relevant state is kept in the client who initiates the RDMA Write request. However, having many outbound RDMA Writes scales poorly as it requires keeping track of $O(n)$ connections for a cluster of n nodes. Thus, HERD sends responses back to the client using the unreliable datagram (UD) transport service. A UD transport allows for one sender queue to issue operations to multiple receive queues (one-to-many pattern). One limitation of the UD transport is that it only supports messaging verbs, RDMA Send and RDMA Receive. HERD thus transmits responses via an RDMA Send in the sender, and the HERD client needs to have pre-issued an RDMA Receive to receive the response message.

7.2.6   HYDRADB

HydraDB is a key-value store that supports high availability by replicating each key-value pair to multiple servers using RDMA [136]. HydraDB partitions the key space in partitions and exclusively assigns a single CPU core to a partition. Get requests in HydraDB are issued as RDMA Reads and are serviced directly without interrupting the remote CPU. Insert and Update requests are issued as messages and are transferred using RDMA Write.

HydraDB couples request detection and dispatch with request processing in a single-threaded execution model. Within a partition, one thread continuously polls the request buffers in a round-robin fashion. When a new request is detected, the thread processes the request and sends the response out via RDMA Write before proceeding to poll the next request buffer. Requests to the same partition will be serialized in the request buffer, but requests to different partitions will be processed concurrently as they are handled by separate threads.

HydraDB supports primary-secondary replication and secondaries do not service client requests. The replication is synchronous and is accelerated using RDMA: each secondary exposes local memory for RDMA operations and the primary issues RDMA Write operations to perform replication. HydraDB monitors the status of all partitions with Zookeeper. If Zookeeper detects a node failure, HydraDB performs reconfiguration by selecting a new primary among the secondaries. If Zookeeper detects a new node joining the network, HydraDB notifies selected partitions to migrate data to the new node.

7.2.7   NESSIE

Nessie is a key-value store that is *serverless*, in that no server process is involved in servicing client requests [21]. The design of Nessie is inspired by the observation that continuously polling at the server is infeasible for environments that cannot dedicate CPU cores exclusively to the key-value store. This requirement is particularly onerous for fast networks where one needs to use a substantial number of CPU cores to utilize the network to its full capacity. By eliminating polling, Nessie is less susceptible to performance degradation caused by interference in shared environments.

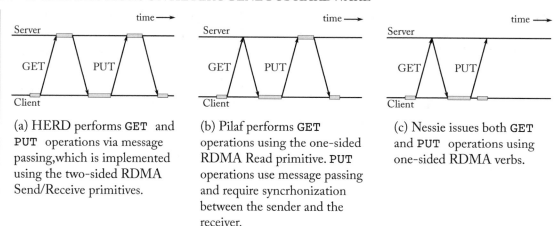

(a) HERD performs **GET** and **PUT** operations via message passing,which is implemented using the two-sided RDMA Send/Receive primitives.

(b) Pilaf performs **GET** operations using the one-sided RDMA Read primitive. **PUT** operations use message passing and require syncrhonization between the sender and the receiver.

(c) Nessie issues both **GET** and **PUT** operations using one-sided RDMA verbs.

Figure 7.4: One-sided operations allow the server to remain passive during operations. HERD, Pilaf, and Nessie differ in which operations are performed in such a manner.

At the storage level, Nessie decouples indexing metadata from key-value pairs. Each instance of Nessie contains an index table, a data table, and a small local cache of remote key-value pairs. Index tables are implemented as cuckoo hash tables. Cuckoo hashing was chosen because it imposes an upper bound on the number of read operations and it is simple to implement without requiring coordination between nodes. Each index table entry is a 64-bit integer, allowing accesses by atomic RDMA CAS verbs. Because CAS verbs are only atomic relative to other RDMA operations on the same NIC, all index table accesses (even for the local index tables) need to be managed using RDMA.

The immutable nature of valid key-value entries allows them to be cached, using their spatially unique index table entry as a cache key. This caching reduces network load, particularly for workloads with skewed popularity distributions. The prototype implementation of Nessie uses a small least recently used (LRU) cache on each node.

CHAPTER 8

Outlook: The Era of Hardware Specialization and Beyond

There are many open challenges ahead for transaction processing. A major challenge is the scalability of transaction processing when databases do not fit in the memory of a single node. This commonly arises with modern Hybrid Transactional-Analytical (HTAP) workloads. Such databases necessitate a scaleable and distributed solution. The problem with scaling transaction processing across a network is that the latency of remote access, even in the fastest networks, is an order of magnitude higher than accessing data in local memory. Making matters worse, many manipulations require multiple round-trips in the network. For transaction processing to scale, it is crucial to overcome the latency of the "network wall" during these operations.

A broader challenge is processing data near the physical point of storage. Although the hardware architecture community has extensively explored how to bring compute closer to DRAM, the bulk of the data will stay in "cold" storage devices for the foreseeable future. The notion of near-data computing thus needs to be expanded to include such devices. Tolerating and recovering from small errors like bit flips is crucial in this environment, and software solutions may have an increasingly bigger role to play in the near future.

Finally, distributed transaction processing naturally raises questions about security and trust among all participating systems. A potential solution can be Blockchain, a distributed ledger technology that is tamper-proof and is appended to by consensus. We highlight some research problems that lie along this path.

8.1 SCALING THE NETWORK WALL FOR DISTRIBUTED TRANSACTION PROCESSING

High-performance networks with Remote Direct Memory Access (RDMA) support are becoming increasingly common. Software developers are facing two unpalatable choices: either communicate using messages and re-implement features of TCP/IP in their application, or find creative ways to cope with the microsecond-long latency of a remote memory access.

Fast, RDMA-capable networks present a "network wall" for data-intensive applications in a data center. Data-intensive applications need better hardware support for remote memory operations in this environment. The hardware already strives to hide the latency of local memory accesses. Existing solutions like simultaneous like multi-threading, prefetching, speculative loading, transactional memory, and configurable coherence domains have been successful in hiding the memory wall from applications, often without even recompiling them. It appears unlikely that hardware improvements alone will be sufficient to scale the "network wall" where latency is 10X higher.

The key technical challenge is that RDMA offers a limited programming interface to remote memory that consists of read, write, and atomic operations. With RDMA alone, completing the most basic operations on either latch-free or latch-based data structures often requires a sequence of remote memory accesses, which translates into multiple round-trips over the network. Transaction processing can benefit from higher-level communication abstractions that support more complex interaction patterns.

8.1.1   A NEW ABSTRACTION: RDMO

This section proposes a new abstraction for data-intensive applications, the Remote Direct Memory Operation (RDMO) interface. The RDMO interface extends the functionality of RDMA by providing a mechanism to simultaneously transmit data and execute simple operations on a remote node. The key idea is that one can augment RDMA to support the dispatch of simple data processing logic in one "unit" to the remote side which will be executed in one round-trip. We term this unit of computation an RDMO. An RDMO is a short sequence of reads, writes, and atomic memory operations that will be transmitted and executed at the remote node without interrupting its CPU, similar to an RDMA operation. Unlike an RPC call, an RDMO cannot invoke program functions, initiate system calls, or issue additional RDMA requests. Unlike a network ISA, an RDMO cannot execute arbitrary user-defined programs.

Consider the common transactional operation of appending a tuple in a slotted page, shown in Figure 8.1a, as an example of a database operation that can be accelerated using RDMOs. A latch-free implementation of this operation would first check if there is enough free space, then atomically modify a pointer to the "free" segment of the page, write the tuple, and finally mark the entry as valid to detect a torn write. Using RDMA, one can only perform this operation on a remote page through a sequence of RDMA requests, as shown in Figure 8.1b. Alternatively, in our system, one can issue a single `SlottedAppend` RDMO, as shown in Figure 8.1c. Overall, an RDMO for inserting a tuple in a slotted page reduces the number of transmitted messages by 4× and reduces latency by as much as 2×. Furthermore, the window of a conflict for the atomic CAS is now reduced by 10×, which allows one order of magnitude more atomic operations to this address. This is one example of how RDMOs can substantially reduce the verbosity of manipulating remote data over a design that solely relies on RDMA. Section 8.1.2 introduces more such examples.

Attributes of RDMOs

The RDMO interface extends conventional send/receive as well as read/write operations. RDMOs are embedded into a larger context of a network interface with the following properties:

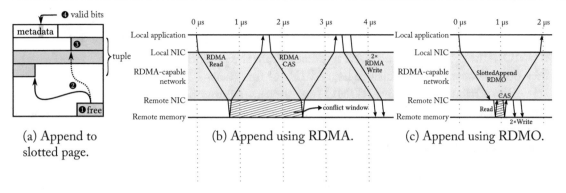

(a) Append to slotted page.   (b) Append using RDMA.   (c) Append using RDMO.

Figure 8.1: A remote direct memory operation (RDMO), dispatches data processing logic to the remote side in one "unit."

Non-Blocking Operations: All functions of the RDMO interface are non-blocking such that the initiator of an operation can interleave communication and computation.

Multithreaded Support: Instead of binding connections to processes, like MPI does, the RDMO interface implements endpoints that are independent of the compute components. An endpoint is a feature-rich extension of a queue pair in InfiniBand. One endpoint can be either shared among multiple threads or exclusively assigned to a single thread, which offers flexibility in application programming.

Quality of Service: Database systems have to support many types of workloads that exhibit different communication patterns and some flows need to be prioritized. The RDMO interface provides QoS functionality using the RDMA QoS semantics. Interfaces like MPI do not offer the option to prioritize different communication flows.

Fault Tolerance: Database systems offer services that must be highly available. The RDMO interface has a clearly defined failure model, inherited by the RDMA interface, that allows applications to react to failures.

Schema Awareness: Database systems operate on structured data. Pushing down schema information to the network enables novel in-network processing applications and operations.

Conditional Operations: Conditional operations allow the developer to evaluate simple *if-then* operations in the remote node. For an RDMO operation with condition check, the remote network card first evaluates if the remote data is in the specified state before applying the operation. This eliminates several round trips and reduces the need for running expensive synchronization or agreement protocols.

8.1.2   FIVE DATABASE RDMOS

This section presents five common operations in database systems that can be accelerated using RDMOs. These operations are used to demonstrate the potential of the RDMO interface and they do not constitute an exclusive list of RDMO functions.

The attributes of the five RDMO functions are summarized in Table 8.1. "Message savings" represents the number of messages saved compared with an RDMA implementation of the same function, if one assumes the same number of scatter/gather entries per request (30) as provided by modern InfiniBand network cards.

Table 8.1: Attributes of RDMO operations

RDMO	Schema Aware?	Conditional?	Message Savings
SlottedAppend	✗	✓	4× or more
ConditionalGather	✓	✓	Up to 30×
SignaledRead	✗	✓	3× or more
WriteAndSeal	✗	✗	2×
ScatterAndAccumulate	✓	✓	Up to 30×

1. SlottedAppend. This operation has been highlighted in Figure 8.1a and corresponds to the common operation of appending a tuple in a buffer. In case of contention, lock conflicts will increase exponentially. Performing this operation as an RDMO shrinks the conflict window and permits more concurrency under contention over an RDMA-only implementation.

2. ConditionalGather. Traversing common data structures often requires following pointers. This requires several lookups over RDMA. This RDMO traverses pointer-based data structures, evaluates a user-defined predicate and gathers the matching elements in a buffer that is transmitted back in a single request. Up to 30 elements (the length of the gather list) can be retrieved in a single RDMO request, instead of one message per element with RDMA.

One example of using this RDMO is in OLTP workloads when reading tuples under multi-version concurrency control, as shown in Figure 8.2a. The `ConditionalGather` RDMO compares timestamps for visibility checking and only returns visible versions in one operation. In an OLAP workload that involves a join, this RDMO retrieves all tuples in a hash bucket that match a key in one round-trip. Short-circuiting the condition to true performs projection in the network.

3. SignaledRead. Many data structures use locks to serialize concurrent operations. Exposing lock-based data structures over RDMA, however, requires at least three RDMA requests: two operations target the lock and one performs the intended operation. This RDMO saves at

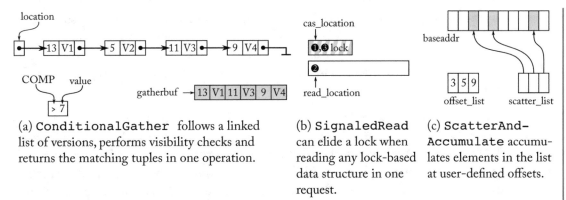

(a) `ConditionalGather` follows a linked list of versions, performs visibility checks and returns the matching tuples in one operation.

(b) `SignaledRead` can elide a lock when reading any lock-based data structure in one request.

(c) `ScatterAnd-Accumulate` accumulates elements in the list at user-defined offsets.

Figure 8.2: Examples using RDMO.

least two messages by "eliding" these lock operations, akin to speculative lock elision in hardware [104].

As shown in Figure 8.2b, the `SignaledRead` RDMO attempts to perform a compare-and-swap operation. If the swap fails, the RDMO retries the compare-and-swap for a few times and then returns the value of the last read. If the swap succeeds, the RDMO reads the requested data and then resets the flag.

4. WriteAndSeal. This RDMO first writes data to a buffer, then writes to the seal location to mark the completion of the write. This would require two messages in an RDMA implementation. This RDMO will be used in lock-based synchronization to update data and release the lock in one operation.

5. ScatterAndAccumulate. This RDMO performs a scatter operation that involves indirect addressing to the destination through a lookup table, as shown in Figure 8.2c. Instead of overwriting the data at the destination, this RDMO accumulates the transmitted values to what is already present in the destination address. `ScatterAndAccumulate` reduces the substantial network cost of hash-based parallel aggregation for high-cardinality domains [80].

8.2   NEAR-DATA TRANSACTION PROCESSING

The end of Dennard scaling has exposed a widening gap between the demand to process ever-growing datasets and the capability of modern computers to do so. In a quest to make data processing faster and more power-efficient, researchers are revisiting the decades-old idea of near data computing which brings computation closer to the data. Transaction processing systems offer a unique approach to the problem.

Near data processing needs to be more than near memory processing.   Pushing some compute capability near or inside DRAM is not sufficient, as cost-benefit analysis shows that it is not economical to keep massive datasets in DRAM. Hence, one needs to look to the next level of the storage hierarchy, currently flash memory, to realize the performance and power benefits of near data computing.

Silent data corruption can be tackled in software.   If the computation is pushed closer to the flash memory chips, the throughput of error-correcting coding (ECC) needs to increase by an order of magnitude. However, the reliability of flash memory cells is deteriorating with technology scaling and more sophisticated ECC codes have prohibitively high implementation complexity. One can no longer assume that the hardware alone will be able to detect and correct data corruption at line rate. A promising solution is to synergistically use software and hardware to make data processing resilient to data corruption.

8.2.1   WHY DATASETS WILL NEVER FIT IN MEMORY: THE "FIVE MINUTE RULE"

A large body of work on near-data computing has focused on in-memory computing, in which logic is added to the memory cell arrays to carry out simple computations. However, it is not economical to store massive datasets in main memory. In a seminal 1987 paper, Jim Gray and Franco Putzolu observed that whether a data item should reside in memory or not is most often a matter of simple cost-benefit analysis [46]. The prescience of the argument still resonates today.

```
In some situations, response time dictates that data be main memory
resident because disc accesses introduce too much delay. These
situations are rare. More commonly, keeping data main-memory resident
is purely an economic issue. When does it make economic sense to
make data resident in main memory? A good rule of thumb is:


                        THE FIVE MINUTE RULE


Data referenced every five minutes should be memory resident.
```

The original rule is inextricably tied to 1980s pricing, but surprisingly, the 5-min rule still holds 30 years after its original publication between DRAM memory and flash memory [5]. In essence, the 5-min rule today says that massive datasets will not be accessed frequently enough to justify the cost of keeping them entirely in DRAM over the much-cheaper flash. This dovetails with the fierce competition among storage vendors to offer affordable all-flash arrays (AFA) for public and private clouds. Fully realizing the performance and power benefits of near data computing requires looking to the next level of the storage hierarchy: bringing compute inside flash-based storage devices.

The data management community has studied how to offload query processing to the microprocessor inside the SSD controller. Recent work has shown that offloading selection and aggregation queries to the SDD improves performance and energy consumption by 3× for a commercial database system [30]. (This work, in turn, builds on Active Disks [109] and Intelligent Disks [60] that exploited the computational power of embedded processors inside spinning hard disks.) The limitation is that the microcontroller inside the SSD device quickly becomes a bottleneck during querying because it is neither powerful nor versatile enough to run general purpose programs. One idea to bypass this limitation calls for using an FPGA between the host and the device for query acceleration [140].

These prior efforts push computation between the host CPU and the flash controller, which means that their data processing capability is limited by the speed of the interface or the flash controller. Bringing computation even closer to the data requires pushing some compute logic below the flash memory controller. This leverages the higher bandwidth between the NAND dies and the flash controller, which is currently underutilized. The challenge with placing compute logic closer to the NAND dies is that computation now needs to be cognizant of the possibility of silent data corruption.

8.2.2 DATA MANAGEMENT OVER UNRELIABLE STORAGE

The reliability of storage media is deteriorating due to technology scaling. As cells shrink, detecting signal over noise becomes harder. In addition, as cells get closer to each other, disturbance errors between neighboring cells are observed [63], and can even break memory isolation between VMs in the cloud [143]. As more bits are packed onto a flash cell, going from single-level flash cells (SLC) to denser MLC and TLC, the voltage differences between levels shrink and flash becomes less reliable. Furthermore, the raw bit error rates (RBER) of SSDs in the field can be one order of magnitude greater than what was predicted in lab tests [118]. These trends suggest that much stronger error-correcting capabilities will be needed in the near future. This is not easy, as ECC decoders already require about 0.5 M gates to keep up with the throughput of NAND flash [52]. Increasing the codeword length is not a solution either, as the decoder complexity increases hyper-linearly with the codeword length. In short, pushing computation below the flash controller would require a much higher transistor and power investment for faster ECC decoding than what the compute logic itself would use! More radical approaches to error detection and correction that transfer part of the work to software are needed.

The data management community is starting to pay more attention to how data corruption can be detected in software. Recent work has proposed software error detection mechanisms that are tailored for in-memory column stores [65]. In this work, error detection is buffered by a data hardening step that encodes the data to make corruption detectable and a data softening step that decodes the data but leaves them vulnerable to corruption. The solution adopts arithmetic coding as a software-based error coding scheme which requires an integer multiplication for data hardening and an integer division for data softening. The appealing feature of arithmetic codes is that they give the database system the ability to directly work on the encoded data representation during query processing. For example, because multiplication is distributive, encoded data can be added directly to compute the encoded sum instead of performing a costly "decode, add, re-encode" sequence in every addition. In essence, arithmetic coding allows for computation to be done before error detection for common numerical operations.

8.2.3   CHALLENGES AND OPPORTUNITIES FOR ERROR CORRECTION

Long BCH or low-density parity-check (LDPC) codes are typical choices for error-correcting codes in SSDs due to their good error-correcting performance and relatively low implementation complexity. Nevertheless, it is very difficult for such decoders to reach a throughput of 30 Gbps or higher, as needed for in-flash data processing. Adopting shorter codes seems essential to reduce the decoding complexity and latency. One could develop decoding strategies that are hierarchical, with lower levels are done in hardware to correct simple errors involving a few bits, and higher levels done in software to catch infrequent multi-bit errors. In addition, the ability to only decode parts of a page would be powerful if combined with *a priori* knowledge of the access pattern and the transaction intent. Things get even more interesting if one considers when is the most appropriate time to check for data corruption when processing a complex query or transaction. Developing error-correcting strategies that jointly optimize the decoder hardware implementation with the database content and transactional workload is a promising open problem.

8.3   BLOCKCHAIN: FAULT-TOLERANT DISTRIBUTED TRANSACTIONS

Blockchain [117, 119, 138] has proven to be a powerful technology with a potential to disrupt a diverse set of applications beyond finance, such as food production [41], energy trading [102], land ownership [100], health care [43], identity management [8], aid delivery [8], insurance fraud prevention [51], and GDPR [25]. This widespread interest is rooted in the fundamental guarantees that blockchain offers, namely, transparency, integrity, and resiliency, all of which must be inalienable data rights of citizens.

In its most basic form, a blockchain is a linked-list of immutable, tamper-proof blocks which are stored at each participating node [47]. Each block records a set of transactions and the associated metadata. Blockchain transactions act on identical ledger data stored at each node. Blockchain was conceived by Satoshi Nakamoto [117] as a peer-to-peer money exchange system. Nakamoto referred to the transactional tokens exchanged among clients in his system as Bitcoins [47].

The emergence of multiple blockchain fabrics [4, 117, 119, 138] has renewed interest in the age-old problem of byzantine fault-tolerant (BFT) consensus (e.g., [22]). BFT consensus guarantees a single replica order consistency across all the non-faulty replicas, even in the presence of byzantine replicas. Public blockchain systems (e.g., [117]) have re-imagined the BFT paradigm using computation-intensive puzzle-solving techniques that arguably result in ineffective use of computational resources. This has motivated practitioners and researchers to rethink traditional communication-intensive BFT algorithms (e.g., [9, 11, 24, 58, 66, 84, 94, 139]), which we envision to flourish in the coming years.

Bibliography

[1] A. Adya, B. Liskov, and P. E. O'Neil. Generalized isolation level definitions. In *Proc. of the 16th International Conference on Data Engineering*, pages 67–78, San Diego, CA, February 28–March 3, 2000. 16

[2] M. K. Aguilera and D. B. Terry. The many faces of consistency. *IEEE Data Engineering Bulletin*, 39(1):3–13, 2016. 9, 16

[3] V. Alvarez, S. Richter, X. Chen, and J. Dittrich. A comparison of adaptive radix trees and hash tables. In *IEEE 31st International Conference on Data Engineering*, pages 1227–1238, April 2015. DOI: 10.1109/icde.2015.7113370 80

[4] E. Androulaki, A. Barger, V. Bortnikov, C. Cachin, K. Christidis, A. De Caro, D. Enyeart, C. Ferris, G. Laventman, Y. Manevich, S. Muralidharan, C. Murthy, B. Nguyen, M. Sethi, G. Singh, K. Smith, A. Sorniotti, C. Stathakopoulou, M. Vukolić, S. W. Cocco, and J. Yellick. Hyperledger Fabric: A distributed operating system for permissioned blockchains. In *Proc. of the 13th EuroSys Conference*, pages 30:1–30:15, ACM, 2018. DOI: 10.1145/3190508.3190538 102

[5] R. Appuswamy, R. Borovica-Gajic, G. Graefe, and A. Ailamaki. The five-minute rule thirty years later and its impact on the storage hierarchy. In *International Workshop on Accelerating Analytics and Data Management Systems Using Modern Processor and Storage Architectures*, pages 1–8, Munich, Germany, September 1, 2017. 100

[6] J. Arulraj, J. J. Levandoski, U. F. Minhas, and P. Larson. BzTree: A high-performance latch-free range index for non-volatile memory. *PVLDB*, 11(5):553–565, 2018. 80

[7] J. Arulraj, A. Pavlo, and P. Menon. Bridging the archipelago between row-stores and column-stores for hybrid workloads. In *Proc. of the International Conference on Management of Data, (SIGMOD)*, pages 583–598, ACM, New York, 2016. 63 DOI: 10.1145/2882903.2915231

[8] GSM Association. Blockchain for development: Emerging opportunities for mobile, identity and aid, 2017. https://www.gsma.com/mobilefordevelopment/progra mme/digital-identity/blockchain-development-emerging-opportunities-mobile-identity-aid/ 102

[9] P.-L. Aublin, S. B. Mokhtar, and V. Quéma. RBFT: Redundant byzantine fault tolerance. In *Proc. of the 33rd International Conference on Distributed Computing Systems, (ICDCS)*, pages 297–306, IEEE Computer Society, 2013. DOI: 10.1109/icdcs.2013.53 67, 103

[10] R. Barber, C. Garcia-Arellano, R. Grosman, R. Müller, V. Raman, R. Sidle, M. Spilchen, A. J. Storm, Y. Tian, P. Tözün, D. C. Zilio, M. Huras, G. M. Lohman, C. Mohan, F. Özcan, and H. Pirahesh. Evolving databases for new-gen big data applications. In *Proc. of the 8th Biennial Conference on Innovative Data Systems Research, (CIDR)*, Chaminade, CA, January 8–11, 2017. 63

[11] J. Behl, T. Distler, and R. Kapitza. Hybrids on steroids: SGX-based high performance BFT. In *Proc. of the 12th European Conference on Computer Systems, (EuroSys)*, pages 222–237, ACM, New York, 2017. DOI: 10.1145/3064176.3064213 103

[12] A. J. Bernstein, D. S. Gerstl, and P. M. Lewis. Concurrency control for step-decomposed transactions. *Information Systems*, 24(9):673–698, December 1999. DOI: 10.1016/s0306-4379(00)00004-1 17

[13] P. A. Bernstein, S. Das, B. Ding, and M. Pilman. Optimizing optimistic concurrency control for Tree-Structured, Log-Structured databases. In *Proc. SIGMOD*, pages 1295–1309, ACM, 2015. DOI: 10.1145/2723372.2737788 19

[14] P. A. Bernstein and N. Goodman. Concurrency control in distributed database systems. *ACM Computing Surveys*, 13(2):185–221, June 1981. DOI: 10.1145/356842.356846 12, 13

[15] P. A. Bernstein, V. Hadzilacos, and N. Goodman. *Concurrency Control and Recovery in Database Systems*. Addison-Wesley Longman Publishing Co., Inc., Boston, MA, 1986. 7, 8, 12, 24

[16] P. A. Bernstein, C. W. Reid, and S. Das. Hyder—A transactional record manager for shared flash. In *5th Biennial Conference on Innovative Data Systems Research, (CIDR)* pages 9–20, Asilomar, CA, January 9–12, 2011. www.cidrdb.org 19

[17] P. A. Bernstein, D. W. Shipman, and W. S. Wong. Formal aspects of serializability in database concurrency control. *IEEE TSE*, SE-5(3):203–216, May 1979. DOI: 10.1109/tse.1979.234182 13

[18] P. A. Boncz, M. Zukowski, and N. Nes. MonetDB/X100: Hyper-pipelining query execution. In *CIDR*, pages 225–237, 2005. 63

[19] E. A. Brewer. Towards robust distributed systems (abstract). In *Proc. of the 19th Annual ACM Symposium on Principles of Distributed Computing, (PODC)*, page 7, New York, 2000. DOI: 10.1145/343477.343502 46

[20] Y. Cao, C. Chen, F. Guo, D. Jiang, Y. Lin, B. C. Ooi, H. T. Vo, S. Wu, and Q. Xu. ES2: A cloud data storage system for supporting both OLTP and OLAP. In *Proc. of the 27th International Conference on Data Engineering, (ICDE)*, pages 291–302, IEEE Computer Society, Washington, DC, 2011. DOI: 10.1109/icde.2011.5767881 62, 63

[21] B. Cassell, T. Szepesi, B. Wong, T. Brecht, J. Ma, and X. Liu. Nessie: A decoupled, client-driven key-value store using RDMA. *IEEE Transactions on Parallel and Distributed Systems*, 28(12):3537–3552, 2017. DOI: 10.1109/tpds.2017.2729545 93

[22] M. Castro and B. Liskov. Practical byzantine fault tolerance. In *Proc. of the 3rd Symposium on Operating Systems Design and Implementation, (OSDI)*, pages 173–186, USENIX Association, Berkeley, CA, 1999. 67, 102

[23] C. Chen, G. Chen, D. Jiang, B. C. Ooi, H. T. Vo, S. Wu, and Q. Xu. Providing scalable database services on the cloud. In *Web Information Systems Engineering, (WISE)*, pages 1–19, Springer, 2010. DOI: 10.1007/978-3-642-17616-6_1 63

[24] B.-G. Chun, P. Maniatis, S. Shenker, and J. Kubiatowicz. Attested append-only memory: Making adversaries stick to their word. In *Proc. of 21st ACM SIGOPS Symposium on Operating Systems Principles, (SOSP)*, pages 189–204, New York, 2007. DOI: 10.1145/1323293.1294280 103

[25] C. Compert, M. Luinetti, and B. Portier. Blockchain and GDPR: How blockchain could address five areas associated with GDPR compliance. *Technical Report*, IBM Security, 2018. 102

[26] B. F. Cooper, A. Silberstein, E. Tam, R. Ramakrishnan, and R. Sears. Benchmarking cloud serving systems with YCSB. In *Proc. SoCC*, pages 143–154, ACM, 2010. DOI: 10.1145/1807128.1807152 66

[27] C. Curino, Y. Zhang, E. P. C. Jones, and S. Madden. Schism: A workload-driven approach to database replication and partitioning. *PVLDB*, 3(1):48–57, 2010. DOI: 10.14778/1920841.1920853 71

[28] C. Diaconu, C. Freedman, E. Ismert, P. Larson, P. Mittal, R. Stonecipher, N. Verma, and M. Zwilling. Hekaton: SQL server's memory-optimized OLTP engine. In *Proc. of the ACM SIGMOD International Conference on Management of Data*, pages 1243–1254, New York, 2013. DOI: 10.1145/2463676.2463710 12, 17, 26, 28, 30, 62, 63, 75

[29] B. Ding, L. Kot, A. Demers, and J. Gehrke. Centiman: Elastic, high performance optimistic concurrency control by watermarking. In *Proc. SoCC*, pages 262–275, ACM, 2015. DOI: 10.1145/2806777.2806837 26

[30] J. Do, Y.-S. Kee, J. M. Patel, C. Park, K. Park, and D. J. DeWitt. Query processing on smart SSDS: Opportunities and challenges. In *Proc. of the ACM SIGMOD International Conference on Management of Data*, pages 1221–1230, New York, 2013. DOI: 10.1145/2463676.2465295 101

[31] A. Dragojevic, D. Narayanan, M. Castro, and O. Hodson. FaRM: Fast remote memory. In *Proc. of the 11th USENIX Symposium on Networked Systems Design and Implementation, (NSDI)*, pages 401–414, Seattle, WA, April 2–4, 2014. 89

[32] A. Eldawy, J. Levandoski, and P. A. Larson. Trekking through Siberia: Managing cold data in a memory-optimized database. *Proc. VLDB Endowment*, 7(11):931–942, July 2014. DOI: 10.14778/2732967.2732968 18

[33] A. J. Elmore, V. Arora, R. Taft, A. Pavlo, D. Agrawal, and A. El Abbadi. Squall: Fine-grained live reconfiguration for partitioned main memory databases. In T. K. Sellis, S. B. Davidson, and Z. G. Ives, Eds., *Proc. of the ACM SIGMOD International Conference on Management of Data*, pages 299–313, Melbourne, Victoria, Australia, May 31–June 4, 2015. DOI: 10.1145/2723372.2723726 73, 74

[34] A. J. Elmore, S. Das, D. Agrawal, and A. E. Abbadi. Zephyr: Live migration in shared nothing databases for elastic cloud platforms. In *Proc. of the ACM SIGMOD International Conference on Management of Data*, pages 301–312, New York, 2011. DOI: 10.1145/1989323.1989356 72

[35] K. P. Eswaran, J. N. Gray, R. A. Lorie, and I. L. Traiger. The notions of consistency and predicate locks in a database system. *Communications of the ACM*, 19(11):624–633, November 1976. DOI: 10.1016/b978-0-934613-53-8.50039-x 13

[36] I. Eyal, A. E. Gencer, E. G. Sirer, and R. Van Renesse. Bitcoin-NG: A scalable blockchain protocol. In *Proc. of the 13th USENIX Conference on Networked Systems Design and Implementation, (NSDI)*, pages 45–59, USENIX Association, Berkeley, CA, 2016. 67

[37] J. M. Faleiro and D. J. Abadi. Rethinking serializable multiversion concurrency control. *Proc. VLDB Endowment*, 8(11):1190–1201, July 2015. DOI: 10.14778/2809974.2809981 45, 49

[38] J. M. Faleiro, D. J. Abadi, and J. M. Hellerstein. High performance transactions via early write visibility. *Proc. VLDB Endowment*, 10(5):613–624, January 2017. DOI: 10.14778/3055540.3055553 48, 49, 50, 52

[39] J. M. Faleiro, A. Thomson, and D. J. Abadi. Lazy evaluation of transactions in database systems. In *Proc. SIGMOD*, pages 15–26, ACM, 2014. DOI: 10.1145/2588555.2610529 46, 49, 52

[40] F. Färber, N. May, W. Lehner, P. Große, I. Müller, H. Rauhe, and J. Dees. The SAP HANA database—an architecture overview. *IEEE Data Engineering Bulletin*, 35(1):28–33, 2012. 12, 45, 63

[41] L. Ge, C. Brewster, J. Spek, A. Smeenk, and J. Top. Blockchain for agriculture and food: Findings from the pilot study. *Technical Report*, Wageningen University, 2017. DOI: 10.18174/426747 102

[42] J. Giceva and M. Sadoghi. Hybrid OLTP and OLAP. In S. Sakr and A. Zomaya, Eds., *Encyclopedia of Big Data Technologies*, pages 1–8, Springer International Publishing, Cham, 2019. https://dblp.org/rec/bib/reference/bdt/GicevaS19 DOI: 10.1007/978-3-319-63962-8_179-1 51, 62

[43] W. J. Gordon and C. Catalini. Blockchain technology for healthcare: Facilitating the transition to patient-driven interoperability. *Computational and Structural Biotechnology Journal*, 16:224–230, 2018. DOI: 10.1016/j.csbj.2018.06.003 102

[44] J. Gray. The transaction concept: Virtues and limitations (invited paper). In *Proc. of the 7th International Conference on Very Large Data Bases*, vol. 7, pages 144–154, VLDB Endowment, 1981. 7, 8

[45] J. Gray, R. A. Lorie, G. R. Putzolu, and I. L. Traiger. Granularity of locks in a large shared data base. In *Proc. of the International Conference on Very Large Data Bases*, pages 428–451, Framingham, MA, September 22–24, 1975. DOI: 10.1145/1282480.1282513 7, 8, 10, 14

[46] J. Gray and F. Putzolu. The 5 minute rule for trading memory for disc accesses and the 10 byte rule for trading memory for CPU time. In *Proc. of the ACM SIGMOD International Conference on Management of Data*, pages 395–398, New York, 1987. DOI: 10.1145/38714.38755 100

[47] S. Gupta and M. Sadoghi. Blockchain transaction processing. In S. Sakr and A. Zomaya, Eds., *Encyclopedia of Big Data Technologies*, pages 1–11, Springer International Publishing, Cham, 2019. https://doi.org/10.1007/978-3-319-63962-8_333-1 DOI: 10.1007/978-3-319-63962-8_333-1 66, 102

[48] S. Gupta and M. Sadoghi. EasyCommit: A non-blocking two-phase commit protocol. In *Proc. of the 21th International Conference on Extending Database Technology, (EDBT)*, pages 157–168, Vienna, Austria, March 26–29, 2018. 45, 62, 66

[49] R. Harding, D. Van Aken, A. Pavlo, and M. Stonebraker. An evaluation of distributed concurrency control. *Proc. VLDB Endowment*, 10(5):553–564, January 2017. DOI: 10.14778/3055540.3055548 66

[50] S. Harizopoulos, D. J. Abadi, S. Madden, and M. Stonebraker.   OLTP through the looking glass, and what we found there.   In *Proc. of the ACM SIGMOD International Conference on Management of Data*, pages 981–992, New York, 2008. DOI: 10.1145/3226595.3226635 74

[51] M. Higginson, J.-T. Lorenz, B. Münstermann, and P. B. Olesen.   The promise of blockchain. *Technical Report*, McKinsey & Company, 2017. 102

[52] K. Ho, C. Chen, and H. Chang. A 520 k (18900, 17010) array dispersion LDPC decoder architectures for NAND flash memory. *IEEE Transactions on Very Large Scale Integration (VLSI) Systems*, 24(4):1293–1304, April 2016. DOI: 10.1109/tvlsi.2015.2464092 101

[53] Z. István, D. Sidler, G. Alonso, and M. Vukolic.   Consensus in a box: Inexpensive coordination in hardware.   In *13th USENIX Symposium on Networked Systems Design and Implementation, (NSDI)*, pages 425–438, Santa Clara, CA, March 16–18, 2016. 84

[54] R. Johnson, I. Pandis, and A. Ailamaki.   Improving OLTP scalability using speculative lock inheritance.   *Proc. VLDB Endowment*, 2(1):479–489, August 2009. DOI: 10.14778/1687627.1687682 31

[55] E. P. C. Jones, D. J. Abadi, and S. Madden. Low overhead concurrency control for partitioned main memory databases. In A. K. Elmagarmid and D. Agrawal, Eds., *SIGMOD Conference*, pages 603–614, ACM, 2010. DOI: 10.1145/1807167.1807233 12, 31, 45

[56] A. Kalia, M. Kaminsky, and D. G. Andersen.   Using RDMA efficiently for key-value services. In *Proc. of the ACM Conference on SIGCOMM*, pages 295–306, New York, 2014. DOI: 10.1145/2619239.2626299 92

[57] R. Kallman, H. Kimura, J. Natkins, A. Pavlo, A. Rasin, S. Zdonik, E. P. C. Jones, S. Madden, M. Stonebraker, Y. Zhang, J. Hugg, and D. J. Abadi.   H-store: A high-performance, distributed main memory transaction processing system. *Proc. VLDB Endowment*, 1(2):1496–1499, August 2008. DOI: 10.14778/1454159.1454211 12, 14, 31, 36, 45, 53, 61, 66

[58] M. Kapritsos et al. All about Eve: Execute-verify replication for multi-core servers. In *Proc. of the 10th USENIX Conference on Operating Systems Design and Implementation, (OSDI)*, pages 237–250, USENIX Association, Berkeley, CA, 2012. 103

[59] G. Karypis and V. Kumar.   A fast and high quality multilevel scheme for partitioning irregular graphs. *SIAM Journal on Scientific Computing*, 20(1):359–392, December 1998. DOI: 10.1137/s1064827595287997 72

[60] K. Keeton, D. A. Patterson, and J. M. Hellerstein. A case for intelligent disks (iDisks). *SIGMOD Record*, 27(3):42–52, September 1998. DOI: 10.1145/290593.290602 101

[61] A. Kemper and T. Neumann. HyPer: A hybrid OLTP & OLAP main memory database system based on virtual memory snapshots. In *Proc. of the 27th International Conference on Data Engineering, (ICDE)*, pages 195–206, IEEE Computer Society, Washington, DC, 2011. DOI: 10.1109/ICDE.2011.5767867 62, 63

[62] K. Kim, T. Wang, R. Johnson, and I. Pandis. ERMIA: Fast memory-optimized database system for heterogeneous workloads. In *Proc. of the International Conference on Management of Data, (SIGMOD)*, pages 1675–1687, ACM, New York, 2016. DOI: 10.1145/2882903.2882905 12, 29, 30

[63] Y. Kim, R. Daly, J. Kim, C. Fallin, J. H. Lee, D. Lee, C. Wilkerson, K. Lai, and O. Mutlu. Flipping bits in memory without accessing them: An experimental study of dram disturbance errors. In *Proc. of the 41st Annual International Symposium on Computer Architecture, (ISCA)*, pages 361–372, IEEE Press, Piscataway, NJ, 2014. DOI: 10.1109/isca.2014.6853210 101

[64] H. Kimura. FOEDUS: OLTP engine for a thousand cores and NVRAM. In *Proc. of the ACM SIGMOD International Conference on Management of Data*, pages 691–706, New York, 2015. DOI: 10.1145/2723372.2746480 12, 55, 57, 66

[65] T. Kolditz, D. Habich, W. Lehner, M. Werner, and S. T. de Bruijn. Ahead: Adaptable data hardening for on-the-fly hardware error detection during database query processing. In *Proc. of the International Conference on Management of Data, (SIGMOD)*, pages 1619–1634, ACM, New York, 2018. DOI: 10.1145/3183713.3183740 101

[66] R. Kotla, L. Alvisi, M. Dahlin, A. Clement, and E. Wong. Zyzzyva: Speculative byzantine fault tolerance. In *Proc. of 21st ACM SIGOPS Symposium on Operating Systems Principles, (SOSP)*, pages 45–58, New York, 2007. DOI: 10.1145/1400214.1400236 67, 103

[67] J. Krueger, C. Kim, M. Grund, N. Satish, D. Schwalb, J. Chhugani, H. Plattner, P. Dubey, and A. Zeier. Fast updates on read-optimized databases using multi-core CPUs. *Proc. VLDB Endowment*, 5(1):61–72, September 2011. DOI: 10.14778/2047485.2047491 63, 64

[68] V. Kumar, Ed. *Performance of Concurrency Control Mechanisms in Centralized Database Systems*. Prentice Hall, Inc., Upper Saddle River, NJ, 1995. 17

[69] H. T. Kung and J. T. Robinson. On optimistic methods for concurrency control. *ACM Transactions on Database Systems*, 6(2):213–226, June 1981. DOI: 10.1109/vldb.1979.718150 15

[70] T. Lahiri, S. Chavan, M. Colgan, D. Das, A. Ganesh, M. Gleeson, S. Hase, A. Holloway, J. Kamp, T.-H. Lee, J. Loaiza, N. Macnaughton, V. Marwah, N. Mukherjee,

A. Mullick, S. Muthulingam, V. Raja, M. Roth, E. Soylemez, and M. Zait. Oracle database in-memory: A dual format in-memory database. In *Proc. of the IEEE 31st International Conference on Data Engineering, (ICDE)*, pages 1253–1258, April 2015. DOI: 10.1109/icde.2015.7113373 62, 63

[71] P. Larson, A. Birka, E. N. Hanson, W. Huang, M. Nowakiewicz, and V. Papadimos. Real-time analytical processing with SQL Server. *Proc. VLDB Endowment*, 8(12):1740–1751, August 2015. DOI: 10.14778/2824032.2824071 63

[72] P. Larson, C. Clinciu, E. N. Hanson, A. Oks, S. L. Price, S. Rangarajan, A. Surna, and Q. Zhou. SQL Server column store indexes. In *Proc. of the ACM SIGMOD International Conference on Management of Data*, pages 1177–1184, New York, 2011. DOI: 10.1145/1989323.1989448 63

[73] P. A. Larson, S. Blanas, C. Diaconu, C. Freedman, J. M. Patel, and M. Zwilling. High-performance concurrency control mechanisms for main-memory databases. *Proc. VLDB Endowment*, 5(4):298–309, December 2011. DOI: 10.14778/2095686.2095689 12, 13, 15, 17, 26, 28

[74] P. L. Lehman and S. B. Yao. Efficient locking for concurrent operations on B-trees. *ACM Transactions on Database Systems*, 6(4):650–670, 1981. DOI: 10.1145/319628.319663 76

[75] V. Leis, A. Kemper, and T. Neumann. The adaptive radix tree: Artful indexing for main-memory databases. In *IEEE 29th International Conference on Data Engineering (ICDE)*, pages 38–49, April 2013. DOI: 10.1109/icde.2013.6544812 79

[76] J. Levandoski, D. Lomet, S. Sengupta, R. Stutsman, and R. Wang. Multi-version range concurrency control in deuteronomy. *Proc. VLDB Endowment*, 8(13):2146–2157, September 2015. DOI: 10.14778/2831360.2831368 68

[77] J. J. Levandoski, D. B. Lomet, and S. Sengupta. The Bw-Tree: A B-tree for new hardware platforms. In *Data Engineering (ICDE), IEEE 29th International Conference on*, pages 302–313, April 2013. DOI: 10.1109/icde.2013.6544834 12, 76

[78] H. Lim, D. Han, D. G. Andersen, and M. Kaminsky. MICA: A holistic approach to fast in-memory key-value storage. In *Proc. of the 11th USENIX Conference on Networked Systems Design and Implementation, (NSDI)*, pages 429–444, USENIX Association, Berkeley, CA, 2014. 91

[79] H. Lim, M. Kaminsky, and D. G. Andersen. Cicada: Dependably fast Multi-Core In-Memory transactions. In *Proc. SIGMOD*, pages 21–35, ACM, 2017. DOI: 10.1145/3035918.3064015 12, 30, 66

[80] F. Liu, A. Salmasi, S. Blanas, and A. Sidiropoulos. Chasing similarity: Distribution-aware aggregation scheduling. *PVLDB*, 12, 2018. 99

[81] D. Lomet, A. Fekete, R. Wang, and P. Ward. Multi-version concurrency via timestamp range conflict management. In *Proc. of the IEEE 28th International Conference on Data Engineering, (ICDE)*, pages 714–725, IEEE Computer Society, Washington, DC, 2012. DOI: 10.1109/icde.2012.10 40, 41

[82] D. Makreshanski, J. Giceva, C. Barthels, and G. Alonso. BatchDB: Efficient isolated execution of hybrid OLTP+OLAP workloads for interactive applications. In *Proc. of the ACM International Conference on Management of Data, (SIGMOD)*, pages 37–50, New York, 2017. DOI: 10.1145/3035918.3035959 67

[83] D. Makreshanski, J. Levandoski, and R. Stutsman. To lock, swap, or elide: On the inter-play of hardware transactional memory and lock-free indexing. *Proc. VLDB Endowment*, 8(11):1298–1309, July 2015. DOI: 10.14778/2809974.2809990 78

[84] A. A. Mamun, T. Li, M. Sadoghi, and D. Zhao. In-memory blockchain: Toward efficient and trustworthy data provenance for HPC Systems. *IEEE International Conference on Big Data*, pages 3808–3813, Big Data, Seattle, WA, December 2018. https://dblp.org/r ec/bib/conf/bigdataconf/MamunLSZ18 103

[85] Y. Mao, E. Kohler, and R. T. Morris. Cache craftiness for fast multicore key-value storage. In *Proc. of the 7th ACM European Conference on Computer Systems (EuroSys)*, pages 183–196, New York, 2012. DOI: 10.1145/2168836.2168855 78

[86] M. M. Michael. Hazard pointers: Safe memory reclamation for lock-free objects. *IEEE Transactions on Parallel and Distributed Systems*, 15(6):491–504, June 2004. DOI: 10.1109/tpds.2004.8 76

[87] M. M. Michael. Scalable lock-free dynamic memory allocation. *SIGPLAN Notices*, 39(6):35–46, June 2004. DOI: 10.1145/2854695.2854697 76

[88] C. Mitchell, Y. Geng, and J. Li. Using one-sided RDMA reads to build a fast, CPU-efficient key-value store. In *Proc. of the USENIX Conference on Annual Technical Confer-ence, (ATC)*, pages 103–114, USENIX Association, Berkeley, CA, 2013. 92

[89] M. Najafi, M. Sadoghi, and H. Jacobsen. Configurable hardware-based streaming ar-chitecture using online programmable-blocks. In J. Gehrke, W. Lehner, K. Shim, S. K. Cha, and G. M. Lohman, Eds., *31st IEEE International Conference on Data Engineer-ing, ICDE*, pages 819–830, IEEE Computer Society, Seoul, South Korea, April 13–17, 2015. DOI: 10.1109/icde.2015.7113336 84

[90] M. Najafi, M. Sadoghi, and H. Jacobsen. A scalable circular pipeline design for multi-way stream joins in hardware. In *34th IEEE International Conference on Data Engineering, (ICDE)*, pages 1280–1283, Paris, France, April 16–19, 2018. DOI: 10.1109/icde.2018.00130

[91] M. Najafi, M. Sadoghi, and H. A. Jacobsen. Flexible query processor on FPGAs. *Proc. VLDB Endowment*, 6(12):1310–1313, August 2013. DOI: 10.14778/2536274.2536303

[92] M. Najafi, M. Sadoghi, and H. A. Jacobsen. The FQP vision: Flexible query processing on a reconfigurable computing fabric. *SIGMOD Record*, 44(2):5–10, August 2015. DOI: 10.1145/2814710.2814712

[93] M. Najafi, K. Zhang, M. Sadoghi, and H. Jacobsen. Hardware acceleration landscape for distributed real-time analytics: Virtues and limitations. In *37th IEEE International Conference on Distributed Computing Systems, (ICDCS)*, pages 1938–1948, Atlanta, GA, June 5–8, 2017. DOI: 10.1109/icdcs.2017.194 84

[94] F. Nawab and M. Sadoghi. Blockplane: A global-scale byzantizing middleware. *IEEE 35th International Conference on Data Engineering (ICDE)*, Macau SAR, April 8–12, 2019. 103

[95] T. Neumann, T. Mühlbauer, and A. Kemper. Fast serializable multi-version concurrency control for main-memory database systems. In *Proc. of the ACM SIGMOD International Conference on Management of Data*, pages 677–689, New York, 2015. DOI: 10.1145/2723372.2749436 12, 28, 62, 63

[96] P. E. O'Neil, E. Cheng, D. Gawlick, and E. J. O'Neil. The log-structured merge-tree (LSM-tree). *Acta Informatica*, 33(4):351–385, 1996. DOI: 10.1007/s002360050048 57

[97] J. Ousterhout, A. Gopalan, A. Gupta, A. Kejriwal, C. Lee, B. Montazeri, D. Ongaro, S. J. Park, H. Qin, M. Rosenblum, S. Rumble, R. Stutsman, and S. Yang. The ramcloud storage system. *ACM Transactions on Computer Systems*, 33(3):7:1–7:55, August 2015. DOI: 10.1145/2806887 88

[98] M. T. Özsu and P. Valduriez. *Principles of Distributed Database Systems*, 3rd ed., Springer, 2011. DOI: 10.1007/978-1-4419-8834-8 66

[99] I. Pandis, R. Johnson, N. Hardavellas, and A. Ailamaki. Data-oriented transaction execution. *Proc. VLDB Endowment*, 3(1–2):928–939, September 2010. DOI: 10.14778/1920841.1920959 34, 49, 52, 66

[100] M. Pisa and M. Juden. Blockchain and economic development: Hype vs. reality. *Technical Report*, Center for Global Development, 2017. 102

[101] H. Plattner. The impact of columnar in-memory databases on enterprise systems: Implications of eliminating transaction-maintained aggregates. *Proc. VLDB Endowment*, 7(13):1722–1729, August 2014. DOI: 10.14778/2733004.2733074 63, 64

[102] PwC. Blockchain—an opportunity for energy producers and consumers?, 2016. https://www.pwc.com/gx/en/industries/assets/pwc-blockchain-opportunity-for-energy-producers-and-consumers.pdf 102

[103] T. Qadah and M. Sadoghi. QueCC: A queue-oriented, control-free concurrency architecture. In *Proc. of the 19th ACM/IFIP/USENIX Middleware Conference*, Rennes, France, December 10–14, 2018. 12, 45, 49, 59, 66

[104] R. Rajwar and J. R. Goodman. Speculative lock elision: Enabling highly concurrent multithreaded execution. In *MICRO*, pages 294–305, 2001. DOI: 10.1109/micro.2001.991127 99

[105] V. Raman, G. Attaluri, R. Barber, N. Chainani, D. Kalmuk, V. KulandaiSamy, J. Leenstra, S. Lightstone, S. Liu, G. M. Lohman, T. Malkemus, R. Mueller, I. Pandis, B. Schiefer, D. Sharpe, R. Sidle, A. Storm, and L. Zhang. DB2 with BLU acceleration: So much more than just a column store. *Proc. VLDB Endowment*, 6(11):1080–1091, August 2013. DOI: 10.14778/2536222.2536233 63

[106] J. Ramnarayan, S. Menon, S. Wale, and H. Bhanawat. SnappyData: A hybrid system for transactions, analytics, and streaming: Demo. In *Proc. of the 10th ACM International Conference on Distributed and Event-based Systems, (DEBS)*, pages 372–373, New York, 2016. DOI: 10.1145/2933267.2933295 64

[107] K. Ren, J. M. Faleiro, and D. J. Abadi. Design principles for scaling multi-core OLTP under high contention. In *Proc. SIGMOD*, pages 1583–1598, ACM, 2016. DOI: 10.1145/2882903.2882958 34, 53

[108] K. Ren, A. Thomson, and D. J. Abadi. Lightweight locking for main memory database systems. *Proc. VLDB Endowment*, 6(2):145–156, December 2012. DOI: 10.14778/2535568.2448947 12, 13, 34, 36, 45, 59

[109] E. Riedel, G. A. Gibson, and C. Faloutsos. Active storage for large-scale data mining and multimedia. In *Proc. of the 24rd International Conference on Very Large Data Bases, (VLDB)*, pages 62–73, Morgan Kaufmann Publishers Inc., San Francisco, CA, 1998. 101

[110] M. Sadoghi, S. Bhattacherjee, B. Bhattacharjee, and M. Canim. L-Store: A real-time OLTP and OLAP system. *CoRR*, abs/1601.04084, 2016. 12, 29, 35, 42, 62, 64, 66

[111] M. Sadoghi, S. Bhattacherjee, B. Bhattacharjee, and M. Canim. L-Store: A real-time OLTP and OLAP system. In *Proc. of the 21th International Conference on Extending Database Technology, (EDBT)*, pages 540–551, Vienna, Austria, March 26–29, 2018. 12, 29, 30, 42, 56, 57, 64, 66

[112] M. Sadoghi, M. Canim, B. Bhattacharjee, F. Nagel, and K. A. Ross. Reducing database locking contention through multi-version concurrency. *Proc. VLDB Endowment*, 7(13):1331–1342, 2014. DOI: 10.14778/2733004.2733006 12, 13, 15, 20, 23, 24, 26, 30, 35, 38, 59, 64, 66

[113] M. Sadoghi and H. Jacobsen. BE-Tree: An index structure to efficiently match Boolean expressions over high-dimensional discrete space. In *Proc. of the ACM SIGMOD International Conference on Management of Data*, pages 637–648, Athens, Greece, June 12–16, 2011. DOI: 10.1145/1989323.1989390 28

[114] M. Sadoghi, M. Labrecque, H. Singh, W. Shum, and H.-A. Jacobsen. Efficient event processing through reconfigurable hardware for algorithmic trading. *Proc. VLDB Endowment*, 3(1–2):1525–1528, September 2010. DOI: 10.14778/1920841.1921029 84

[115] M. Sadoghi, K. A. Ross, M. Canim, and B. Bhattacharjee. Making updates disk-I/O friendly using SSDs. *Proc. VLDB Endowment*, 6(11):997–1008, August 2013. DOI: 10.14778/2536222.2536226 12, 20, 21, 28, 29, 35, 43, 64

[116] M. Sadoghi, K. A. Ross, M. Canim, and B. Bhattacharjee. Exploiting SSDs in operational multiversion databases. *VLDB Journal*, 25(5):651–672, 2016. DOI: 10.1007/s00778-015-0410-5 12, 20, 21, 22, 28, 29, 35, 43, 64

[117] N. Satoshi. Bitcoin: A peer-to-peer electronic cash system, 2008. https://bitcoin.org/bitcoin.pdf https://bitcoin.org/en/bitcoin-paper 67, 102, 103

[118] B. Schroeder, R. Lagisetty, and A. Merchant. Flash reliability in production: The expected and the unexpected. In *14th Conference on File and Storage Technologies (FAST)*, pages 67–80, USENIX Association, Santa Clara, CA, 2016. 101

[119] D. Schwartz, N. Youngs, and A. Britto. The Ripple Protocol Consensus Algorithm, 2014. https://ripple.com/files/ripple_consensus_whitepaper.pdf 102

[120] M. Serafini, R. Taft, A. J. Elmore, A. Pavlo, A. Aboulnaga, and M. Stonebraker. Clay: Fine-grained adaptive partitioning for general database schemas. *PVLDB*, 10(4):445–456, 2016. DOI: 10.14778/3025111.3025125 74

[121] D. Shasha, F. Llirbat, E. Simon, and P. Valduriez. Transaction chopping: Algorithms and performance studies. *ACM Transactions on Database Systems*, 20(3):325–363, September 1995. DOI: 10.1145/211414.211427

[122] R. Shaull, L. Shrira, and H. Xu. Skippy: A new snapshot indexing method for time travel in the storage manager. In *Proc. of the ACM SIGMOD International Conference on Management of Data*, pages 637–648, New York, 2008. DOI: 10.1145/1376616.1376681 12

[123] V. Sikka, F. Färber, W. Lehner, S. K. Cha, T. Peh, and C. Bornhövd. Efficient transaction processing in SAP HANA database: The end of a column store myth. In *Proc. of the ACM SIGMOD International Conference on Management of Data*, pages 731–742, New York, 2012. DOI: 10.1145/2213836.2213946 12, 64

[124] M. Stonebraker, D. J. Abadi, A. Batkin, X. Chen, M. Cherniack, M. Ferreira, E. Lau, A. Lin, S. Madden, E. O'Neil, P. O'Neil, A. Rasin, N. Tran, and S. Zdonik. C-store: A column-oriented DBMS. In *Proc. of the 31st International Conference on Very Large Data Bases, (VLDB)*, pages 553–564, VLDB Endowment, 2005. DOI: 10.1145/3226595.3226638 63

[125] M. Stonebraker and A. Weisberg. The VoltDB main memory DBMS. *IEEE Data Engineering Bulletin*, 36(2):21–27, 2013. 62

[126] D. Tang, H. Jiang, and A. J. Elmore. Adaptive concurrency control: Despite the looking glass, one concurrency control does not fit all. In *CIDR*, 2017. 59

[127] A. Thomasian. Concurrency control: Methods, performance, and analysis. *ACM Computing Surveys*, 30(1):70–119, March 1998. DOI: 10.1145/274440.274443 17

[128] A. Thomson and D. J. Abadi. The case for determinism in database systems. *Proc. VLDB Endowment*, 3(1):70–80, 2010. DOI: 10.14778/1920841.1920855 12, 45

[129] A. Thomson, T. Diamond, S. C. Weng, K. Ren, P. Shao, and D. J. Abadi. Calvin: Fast distributed transactions for partitioned database systems. In *Proc. SIGMOD*, pages 1–12, ACM, 2012. DOI: 10.1145/2213836.2213838 12, 34, 45, 66

[130] TPC-C, on-line transaction processing benchmark. http://www.tpc.org/tpcc/ 66

[131] S. Tu, W. Zheng, E. Kohler, B. Liskov, and S. Madden. Speedy transactions in multicore in-memory databases. In *Proc. of the 24th ACM Symposium on Operating Systems Principles, (SOSP)*, pages 18–32, New York, 2013. DOI: 10.1145/2517349.2522713 12

[132] S. Tu, W. Zheng, E. Kohler, B. Liskov, and S. Madden. Speedy transactions in multicore in-memory databases. In *SOSP*, pages 18–32, ACM, 2013. DOI: 10.1145/2517349.2522713 53, 57, 59, 66, 78

[133] T. Wang, R. Johnson, A. Fekete, and I. Pandis. The serial safety net: Efficient concurrency control on modern hardware. In *Proc. of the 11th International Workshop*

on Data Management on New Hardware, (DaMoN), New York, ACM, 2015. DOI: 10.1145/2771937.2771949 29, 41

[134] T. Wang and H. Kimura. Mostly-optimistic concurrency control for highly contended dynamic workloads on a thousand cores. *Proc. VLDB Endowment*, 10(2):49–60, October 2016. DOI: 10.14778/3015274.3015276 12, 13, 57, 66

[135] T. Wang, J. Levandoski, and P.-Å. Larson. Easy lock-free indexing in non-volatile memory. *34th IEEE International Conference on Data Engineering ICDE*, pages 461–472, Paris, France, April 2018. https://dblp.org/rec/bib/conf/icde/WangLL18 DOI: 10.1109/icde.2018.00049 81

[136] Y. Wang, L. Zhang, J. Tan, M. Li, Y. Gao, X. Guerin, X. Meng, and S. Meng. HydraDB: A resilient RDMA-driven key-value middleware for in-memory cluster computing. In *Proc. of the International Conference for High Performance Computing, Networking, Storage and Analysis, (SC)*, pages 22:1–22:11, New York, ACM, 2015. DOI: 10.1145/2807591.2807614 93

[137] Z. Wang, S. Mu, Y. Cui, H. Yi, H. Chen, and J. Li. Scaling multicore databases via constrained parallel execution. In *Proc. SIGMOD*, pages 1643–1658, ACM, 2016. DOI: 10.1145/2882903.2882934

[138] G. Wood. Ethereum: A secure decentralised generalised transaction ledger, 2015. https://gavwood.com/paper.pdf 102

[139] T. Wood, R. Singh, A. Venkataramani, P. Shenoy, and E. Cecchet. ZZ and the art of practical BFT execution. In *Proc. of the 6th Conference on Computer Systems, (EuroSys)*, pages 123–138, New York, ACM, 2011. DOI: 10.1145/1966445.1966457 103

[140] L. Woods, Z. István, and G. Alonso. Ibex: An intelligent storage engine with support for advanced SQL offloading. *Proc. VLDB Endowment*, 7(11):963–974, July 2014. DOI: 10.14778/2732967.2732972 101

[141] L. Wu, A. Lottarini, T. K. Paine, M. A. Kim, and K. A. Ross. Q100: The architecture and design of a database processing unit. In *Architectural Support for Programming Languages and Operating Systems, (ASPLOS)*, pages 255–268, Salt Lake City, UT, March 1–5, 2014. DOI: 10.1145/2541940.2541961 85

[142] L. Wu, A. Lottarini, T. K. Paine, M. A. Kim, and K. A. Ross. The Q100 database processing unit. *IEEE Micro*, 35(3):34–46, 2015. DOI: 10.1109/mm.2015.51 85

[143] Y. Xiao, X. Zhang, Y. Zhang, and R. Teodorescu. One bit flips, one cloud flops: Cross-VM row hammer attacks and privilege escalation. In *25th Security Symposium*, pages 19–35, USENIX Association, Austin, TX, 2016. 101

[144] C. Yao, D. Agrawal, G. Chen, Q. Lin, B. C. Ooi, W. F. Wong, and M. Zhang. Exploiting single-threaded model in multi-core in-memory systems. *IEEE TKDE*, 28(10):2635–2650, 2016. DOI: 10.1109/tkde.2016.2578319 45, 46, 49

[145] X. Yu, G. Bezerra, A. Pavlo, S. Devadas, and M. Stonebraker. Staring into the abyss: An evaluation of concurrency control with one thousand cores. *Proc. VLDB Endowment*, 8(3):209–220, November 2014. DOI: 10.14778/2735508.2735511 14

[146] X. Yu, A. Pavlo, D. Sanchez, and S. Devadas. TicToc: Time traveling optimistic concurrency control. In *Proc. SIGMOD*, pages 1629–1642, ACM, 2016. DOI: 10.1145/2882903.2882935 12, 37, 38, 40, 41, 66

[147] Y. Yuan, K. Wang, R. Lee, X. Ding, J. Xing, S. Blanas, and X. Zhang. BCC: Reducing false aborts in optimistic concurrency control with low cost for in-memory databases. *Proc. VLDB Endowment*, 9(6):504–515, January 2016. DOI: 10.14778/2904121.2904126 31

[148] K. Zhang, K. Wang, Y. Yuan, L. Guo, R. Lee, and X. Zhang. Mega-KV: A case for GPUs to maximize the throughput of in-memory key-value stores. *PVLDB*, 8(11):1226–1237, 2015. DOI: 10.14778/2809974.2809984 86

[149] X. Zhou, X. Zhou, Z. Yu, and K. L. Tan. Posterior snapshot isolation. In *IEEE 33rd International Conference on Data Engineering (ICDE)*, pages 797–808, April 2017. DOI: 10.1109/icde.2017.130 38, 40, 41

Authors' Biographies

MOHAMMAD SADOGHI

Mohammad Sadoghi is an Assistant Professor in the Computer Science Department at the University of California, Davis. Formerly, he was an Assistant Professor at Purdue University. Prior to joining academia, he was a Research Staff Member at IBM T.J. Watson Research Center for nearly four years. He received his Ph.D. from the Computer Science Department at the University of Toronto in 2013. At UC Davis, Prof. Sadoghi leads the *ExpoLab* research group with the aim to pioneer a new exploratory data platform—referred to as *ExpoDB*—a distributed ledger that unifies secure transactional and real-time analytical processing, all centered around a democratic and decentralized computational model.

He has over 60 publications in the leading database conferences and journals (e.g., SIG-MOD, VLDB, ICDE, Middleware, ATC, EDBT, TODS, and TKDE) and has filed 34 U.S. patents. His SIGMOD'11 paper, "BE-Tree: An index structure to efficiently match Boolean expressions over high-dimensional discrete space," was awarded EPTS Innovative Principles Award; his EDBT'11 paper, "GPX-Matcher: A generic Boolean predicate-based XPath expression matcher," was selected as one of the best EDBT papers in 2011; his ESWC'16 paper entitled "Predicting Drug-Drug Interactions through Large-Scale Similarity-Based Link Prediction" won the Best In-Use Paper Award; and his Middleware'18, "QueCC: A Queue-oriented, Control-free Concurrency Architecture," won the Best Paper Award. He has presented a tutorial at ICDE'16 on "Accelerating Database Workloads by Software-Hardware-System Co-design."

He has served as the General Co-Chair of ACM/IFIP Middleware'19, the PC Chair (Industry Track) for ACM DEBS'17; initiated and co-chaired Active Series workshops at ICDE'17, Middleware'17, ICDE'18, ICDE'19; co-chaired the Doctoral Symposium at ACM/IFIP/USENIX Middleware'17; served as Workshop/Tutorial Co-chair at Middleware'18. He regularly serves on the program committee of SIGMOD, VLDB, Middleware, ICDE, EDBT, ICDCS, and ICSOC; and has been an invited reviewer for TKDE, TPDS, and VLDBJ.

SPYROS BLANAS

Spyros Blanas is an Assistant Professor in the Department of Computer Science and Engineering at The Ohio State University since 2014. He received his Ph.D. at the University of Wisconsin–Madison, where he was a member of the Database Systems group and the Microsoft Jim Gray Systems Lab. Part of his Ph.D. dissertation was commercialized in Microsoft SQL Server 2014 as the Hekaton in-memory transaction processing engine. His research interest is high-performance database systems and his current goal is to build a data management system for high-end computing facilities. Prof. Blanas has published in leading database and systems conferences (e.g. SIGMOD, VLDB, EuroSys, SoCC) and his research contributions have been recognized with the IEEE TCDE Rising Star award. This year he is the PC vice-chair for transaction processing for ICDE'18. He regularly serves on the program committees of SIGMOD, VLDB, ICDE, SoCC, SSDBM, CIKM; he has been reviewing for the *VLDB Journal, IEEE TKDE, IEEE TPDS, ACM TODS,* and the *SIGMOD Record.*

Printed in the United States
by Baker & Taylor Publisher Services